Ed. No. WE3

# *PULSE*
## *A HISTORY OF MUSIC*
## *by*
## *Lena McLin*

D1568047

*Neil A. Kjos Music Co. Distributor*
*Park Ridge & San Diego*

© 1977 KJOS West    San Diego, California

Published by Kjos West

Distributed by Neil A. Kjos Music Company

National Order Desk

4382 Jutland Drive, San Diego, California 92117

International Standard Book Number 0-8497-5600-6

Library of Congress Card Number 77-75478

Printed and Bound in the United States of America

Edition Number WE3

# *Table of Contents*

## MODERN AMERICA—Country, Folk, Blues and Gospel

## MODERN AMERICA—Rock

## THE PULSE

# List of Illustrations

# Introduction

When you hear the word "Music", it stirs up associations with your own personal musical involvements. If your involvements have been limited, then your musical awareness probably has been restricted. Have you ever considered that *Music Is the Sum Total of Man's Life Experiences?*

People, through the pulse of their music, speak to us about their —

1. Life styles (we can call this their culture);
2. Fantasy adventures, personal challenges and desires;
3. Themselves, friends, family, or heroes;
4. Fears and apprehensions about things for which they can or cannot find answers: nature, disease, climate, love, fate;
5. Ceremonies which celebrate or relate to all of the aspects of their heritage and their life and death (religion).

This is why we want to expand our own musical knowledge and involvements. Through music, we can create a vivid and more compassionate understanding of our people and our art.

**Lena McLin**

# The Earliest American Musicians

# THE EARLIEST
# AMERICAN MUSICIANS

There are few traces of the music of the earliest Americans in the music you are likely to hear today. But they did have music. We know this because their musical instruments survived. Through their instruments, we can trace their migration from Siberia which is now part of the Soviet Union. That was more than 8,000 years ago. Indian tribes of North, Central and South America still play some of these instruments. The Eskimo Indians settled in Alaska where they have remained to this day.

Much of the music of the Earliest Americans remained within their tribes. It was used to remember historical facts, social conditions, life styles, customs and religion. Their music also included singing, chanting and dances.

The system of writing music as we know it today was not known to these Americans. They used their own system of notation. One system made use of figures. The figures were characters which represented certain tones or musical phrases. This character notation helped the singer recall the ideas he had already learned.

Because the Earliest Americans and the New Arrivals from England were not allowed to socialize, the Earliest Americans were thought of as enemies. Citizenship rights and educational opportunities for the Earliest Americans were neglected. This isolation and rejection led to a lack of appreciation of the cultural value of the Earliest Americans by the New Arrivals.

Modern Americans may not remember that the Iroquois Confederacy (of Indian Nations), which was held around 1570 in what is now the Northeastern United States, was one of the world's greatest social movements. Its Constitution is said to have influenced the writing of the United States Constitution. The Iroquois Constitution is preserved today in the Archives of New York State.

Music that has become part of todays music has its roots in Europe and Africa. It came to America with the New Arrivals.

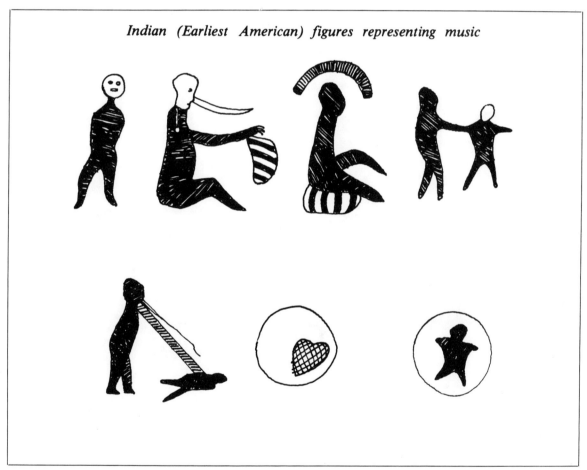

*Indian (Earliest American) figures representing music*

## RECALL

1. The Earliest Americans arrived from Siberia more than _____ years ago.

2. The _____ _____ followed, settling in Alaska where they live today.

3. Much of the music of the Earliest Americans remained within their _____.

4. The Earliest Americans and the New Arrivals from _____ were not allowed to socialize.

5. A system of writing music using _____ was used by the Earliest Americans.

6. We can trace the migration of the Earliest Americans through their _____, many of which are still played.

# EUROPE

# The Baroque Period in Music & History 1600-1750

# EUROPE

## The Baroque Period in Music 1600-1750

In Europe during the late sixteenth century, when America was under exploration and colonization, musicians, poets and scholars wanted to explore new artistic directions and new musical sounds. One of the most important cultural centers was in the Italian city of Florence. There, a group known as the "Florentine Camerata" met regularly to create and develop new ideas and trends in music, art and drama.

The Baroque ("Bar-rohk") Period saw the development of the following musical characteristics:

1. Music written or based on major or minor harmony (tonal center).
2. A one voice melodic lead supported by chords (homophony).
3. Prominence of religious texts or subjects.
4. Predominance of the harpsicord.
5. An orchestra primarily composed of strings with a few woodwinds.
6. The figured bass (Bass Continuo)(the writing out of the bass line in numbers).
7. Very ornamental melodies which never seemed to end but were like evolving, continuous ideas.
8. Relentless and pulsating rhythms.
9. One mood or one thought throughout a composition.

Some musical forms of the Baroque Period:

Vocal: aria, arioso, accompanied solo song, recitative, opera, oratorio, cantata;

Instrumental: dance suite, solo sonata, trio sonata, solo concerto, concerto grosso (concertino and ripieni), overture, fugue, prelude.

During the Baroque Period, musicians were thought of in the same social class as servants. They belonged to and received their musical training from "Guilds." The Guilds had three stages:

1. Apprentice — Members were allowed to live with master-musicians (without pay) in exchange for being given musical training. The apprentice often learned trades such as how to repair instruments and how to copy music.

2. Journeyman — This was a period during which the student traveled, often to various countries, in order to study with other great composers, musicians and master teachers.

3. Master Musician — This final stage represented the end of the student's musical studies and the beginning of his professional career ( he could obtain a position as a Master Musician). Master Musicians were hired by the clergy or the aristocracy (ruling class).

## The Baroque Period in History 1600-1750

This was the era that laid the foundation for today's concert music. Some events occurring during the Baroque Period were:

Germany—The Thirty Years War

America—The Opening of the American Frontier

China and India—Trading started with Europe

Spain and France—Revolt from the Netherlands—Religious feeling was very strong.

The Protestant revolution replaced the Roman Catholic faith with protestant beliefs in many countries.

The Church and State were becoming separated.

### CLAUDIO MONTEVERDI 1567-1643

Claudio Monteverdi, an Italian opera composer, can be compared with the greatest opera composers because of his powerful and dramatic compositions. His understanding of life during the Baroque Period introduced and brought to the world of opera many advanced characterizations. Monteverdi was also the first composer to write special parts for each instrument in the orchestra. The singers could no longer expect the instruments to play along with them on exactly the same musical lines, themes or melodies. He created a completely independent accompaniment which made opera more interesting.

### ARCANGELO CORELLI 1653-1713

Arcangelo Corelli was one of the early developers of the Sonata form (Exposition—Development—Recapitulation). He composed music in several parts to be played by from one to three instruments. He organized the early attempts at using musical form in a definite musical style. These compositions were called church sonatas.

Many composers were to follow Corelli's form. He was also a master of the violin and helped to establish the style of writing for the violin.

### ANTONIO VIVALDI 1675-1741

Antonio Vivaldi was another Italian master composer, violinist and teacher. He was a student of Corelli and was greatly influenced by him. Vivaldi is credited with the standardization of the "concerto grosso" form.

In the "concerto grosso," a small group of instruments with soft, light sounds and timbres (called the concertino) is set against a larger group of brighter, louder instruments (called the ripieni). These two groups then alternate playing. This popular Baroque Period form is like a musical contest between the concertino and the ripieno groups.

Vivaldi, in his position as musical director of the Conservatory of Pieta in Venice, frequently wrote music for the orchestra using the concerto and sonata forms. As a trend maker, Vivaldi paved the way for use of "programmatic" music which would become popular during the later Romantic Period. "Program" music imitates, describes, or tells a story (narrative).

These principles are reflected in his masterful concerto, "Four Seasons," where winter, spring, summer and fall are vividly portrayed.

**RECALL**

1. Claudio Monteverdi, the opera composer, can be compared with the greatest _____ _____.

2. Monteverdi was the first composer to write _____ _____ for the instruments of the orchestra.

3. Antonio Vivaldi is credited with standardizing the _____ form.

4. Vivaldi paved the way for the use of _____ _____.

## JOHANN SEBASTIAN BACH
### 1685-1750

Johann Sebastian Bach was born in Eisenach, Saxony (Germany), where his father was a violinist and taught him to play the violin. So many Bachs in this area of Germany became musicians that everyone who was musical at all was thought to be a Bach.

For more than two hundred and fifty years beginning in the Baroque Period, Bachs dominated the musical scene. Some were in town instrumental groups, others in church musical organizations and others were just amateur musicians.

When J.S. Bach was ten, he had to move in with his brother because of the death of his parents. His brother taught him to play the harpsichord and organ.

At fifteen, Bach was a singer in a choir at Luneberg, Germany. When his voice changed, his ability to play the keyboard saved his job. He is known to have held positions as both violinist and organist. Bach had an intense interest in music, and it is said that he once walked over two hundred miles to hear the famed organist, Buxtehude. Bach had twenty children from his two marriages. He loved all of them very much and is written of as a devoted father. In 1723, Bach was appointed Cantor-Musical Director in Leipzig at the St. Thomas School where he remained until his death in 1750. In Leipzig, Bach began the development of the tempered musical scale. Music of the earlier periods had been restricted to limited scales. Bach expanded the scales and tempered (adjusted) the tones of the clavichord so that they sounded better when played together or in sequences. The tempered scale is still used in most of our music to this day.

Bach also gave private lessons to students and wrote his *Preludes and Fugues* for thirty keys (fifteen major keys and fifteen minor keys). His students had to master these *Preludes and Fugues* for the tempered scale clavichord. Piano students today still try to master the phenomenal "Preludes and Fugues" of the *Well-Tempered Clavichord* by Johann Sebastian Bach.

J.S. Bach is considered one of the most important musicians and composers ever to have lived. His works include: two hundred cantatas (sacred narratives) including the famous Easter Cantata, *Christ Lag in Todesbanden* (Christ Lay by Death Enshrouded) — most of his cantatas are about twenty five to thirty minutes; five Passions (Biblical stories of Christ) including the famous *St. Matthew's Passion*; the *B-Minor Mass*; one hundred forty organ Chorales — the best loved settings of hymn tunes of the time; fifty organ Fugues including the famous *Toccata and*

*Fugue in C-Minor;* the *Wohltemperiertes Clavier* (Well-Tempered Clavichord) which consists of two sets of Preludes and Fugues from all major and minor keys; the *Goldberg Variations* — a piece earlier known as the *Aria with Thirty Variations; the Brandenberg Concertos,* consisting of six concertos; four Overtures presently called Orchestral Suites — two of the most popular today are *Suite No. 2 in B-Minor* and *Suite No. 3 in D-Minor* which contains the *Air for the G String;* and finally, his last great composition, *The Art of the Fugue.*

## RECALL

1. Johann Sebastian Bach's father taught him to play the _____.
2. His brother taught him to play the _____ and _____.
3. Bach was appointed Cantor-Musical Director in _____ where he remained until his death in 1750.

4. In Leipzig, Bach began the development of the _____ _____ _____.
5. J.S. Bach is considered one of the most important musicians and _____ ever to have lived.
6. Name one of the J.S. Bach's compositions you remember best: _____.

## GEORG FREDRICH HANDEL
## 1658-1759

Georg Friedrich Handel was born in Halle, Saxony, on February 23, 1685. His parents planned for him to study law. Responding to Handel's unusual interest in music, an older friend was able to have a harpsichord placed in the attic of the Handel home when Georg was only eight years old. There, Handel secretly taught himself to play the harpsichord.

Friends of Handel's father, who recognized the boy's talent, convinced his father to let the young man study with a local organist, Zachau. He studied composition, counterpoint (the art of interweaving melody) and four instruments: oboe, clavichord, organ and violin. Labeled a child prodigy by the time he was eleven, he had mastered the music courses and instruments Zachau had taught so well that the organist was convinced there was no longer any help that he could give his student.

Handel traveled to Berlin where at the age of nineteen he wrote and produced four operas. Between 1707 and 1710 Handel lived in Italy where he wrote many works including two oratorios and two operas. He then went to England where he had successes with the two operas, *Teseo* and *Rinaldo.*

Georg I, before he became King of England, was known as the Elector of Hanover (Germany). He became Handel's Patron (a financial supporter). Georg I was angered with Handel at that time for writing music for the Church of England in English because it was usually written in Latin. But, after he became King of England, and Handel wrote the now famous *Water Music* for the King's Water Festival on the River Thames, he forgot his displeasure.

After an unhappy experience as co-director of an opera company at the Royal Academy of Music in London, Handel founded his own Opera Company. This Company eventually failed although Handel wrote thirteen years for the Company.

Following a partially paralyzing stroke in 1737, Handel began to write oratorios. He produced his *Passion Oratorio* in Berlin in 1740. The *Messiah,* the most famous of all his works, tells about Christ — the prophecy of Christ and his birth, death and resurrection. The text of the *Messiah,* which Handel edited, was by Charles Jennens. The *Messiah* was performed with Handel conducting during a concert tour in Dublin, Ireland in 1742.

Handel wrote very rapidly. For example, it took only twenty-one days to write the entire *Messiah*. During the singing of the *Hallelujah Chorus*, the King was so impressed that he stood. Since that time, it has become traditional to stand during the singing of the *Hallelujah Chorus*.

Handel completely lost his sight six years before he died. he made his last public performance at the Covent Garden, London's famous musical center, on April 6, 1759. His blindness, along with his paralysis, did not hinder his great organ playing. From the year 1715 until he died in 1759, the British Court paid Handel's salary because the English people adored him.

His lasting impression on the history of music fills many, many volumes. His writings cover many musical forms.

He is buried in Westminster Abbey in London. Handel never married.

## RECALL

1. Georg Frederic Handel **secretly taught himself** to play the _____.

2. He studied composition and counterpoint and learned to play the _____, _____, _____ and viola.

3. The "_____" is the most famous of all Handel's works.

4. The _____ _____ paid Handel's salary because the English people adored him.

5. Handel is buried in _____ _____ in London.

6. Name a work by Handel you remember best: _____.

# AMERICA
# 1600-1750

# AMERICA 1600-1750

## A Union of Many

The year 1619 saw small numbers of New Arrivals coming to America from other countries. They left Europe in its early Baroque Period and settled into various colonies in America. All of these New Arrivals, or Colonists, including indentured servants and slaves, were totally involved in the problem of survival. The newly arrived Colonists were frequently at war with the Earliest Americans.

There were understandably few musical instruments among the Colonists, although they did bring drums, trumpets, bells, and later, jew's harps. The jew's harp was often used for trading with the Earliest Americans while the bells, drums and trumpets were used for calling church services, emergencies and warnings of attacks.

Most of the instruments belonged to the wealthier people of the colonies. Folk music, both sacred and secular, was of course, brought from the home countries. Very little, if any, early music was available in written form. The performer, for the most part, had to rely on his memory. The people of the colonies played and sang ballads, sea chanties, folk songs and lullabyes, as well as humorous nonsense ditties.

The settlers from England had been accustomed to a singing country where educated people, the so-called cultured citizens, followed the style of playing a musical instrument and singing. The only time that the colonists used music together was during their church services and for very special functions (funerals, marriages, birthdays, etc.). The music used in the church came from hymn books brought over by the early settlers. These hymn books continued to undergo changes with each new generation.

In 1612, Henry Ainsworth arranged the *Ainsworth Book of Psalms* for the separatists (Pilgrims) who left England and went to Holland. When the Pilgrims came from Holland to America in 1620, they brought it with them. This book remained in use until about 1692.

### RECALL

1. The year 1619 saw small numbers of New Arrivals coming to America from other countries. They settled into various

_____.

2. The Colonists were frequently at war with the

_____.

3. There were few musical instruments among these colonists, although they did have

_____, _____,

_____ and the _____

_____ which they often traded with the Earliest Americans.

4. Most of the instruments belonged to the

_____ people of the colonies.

5. The settlers from _____ were accustomed to a singing country.

6. The only time that the colonists used music together was during their _____

_____ and for very

_____ _____.

7. The music used in the church came from

_____ _____ brought over by the early settlers.

8. In 1612 Henry Ainsworth arranged
"_____ _____

_____ _____."

## THE PURITANS

The Puritans were New Arrivals to America around 1630. They brought with them a different hymn book, *The Sternhold-Hopkins Book* (and probably the *Ainsworth Psalm Book*).

The *Sternhold-Hopkins Book* proved to be a problem since the English text did not fit the music. A committee was formed to prepare a new translation and put the Psalms into English meter. This new book was called the *Whole Booke of Psalmes.*

The *Whole Booke of Psalmes* was the first book to be printed in the colonies. It was printed by the Stephen Day Press in Cambridge, Massachusetts in 1640, ten years after the arrival of the Puritans. The printing press had been sent from England to America in 1638 as a gift from the Dutch citizens sympathetic to the Puritans.

The early editions of the *Whole Booke of Psalmes* contained no music. However, the ninth edition of this book included printed melodies using shaped notes.

Shaped Notes

fa    sol    la    mi

Since this English fa-sol-la-mi System used only four syllables, they had to be repeated in order to sing a complete scale. The Puritans' music used a quick and lively tempo.

A tune that is still familiar to many today was taken from the *Ainsworth Psalter*. It is called *Old Hundredth* or *Doxology* and is often referred to as *Praise God, From Whom All Blessings Flow*. Several composers have been given credit for this tune, among them J. Dowland, Martin Luther and Louis Bourgeois.

The religious denomination of the Puritans was Congregational. To train their future leaders, they founded the first college in America, Harvard, in 1636 (today Harvard University). Music was very much a part of the College's educational training.

## HYMN SINGING IN THE CHURCH

In England (Great Britain), the Parish clerk had the task of being the songleader. He outlined the hymn tune for the congregation. The songleader would usually sing the song, line by line, waiting after each line for the congregation to repeat the line he had just finished. The settlers continued this English practice of having a songleader. In New England, this job was given to the Deacon, who was called the Precentor.

Often the singing was very poor and songs were pitched too low or too high. Many Precentors added their own versions of the tunes. Toward the end of the seventeenth century, there was much unrest and confusion about many of the tunes. The clergy saw a need for improving the singing and the way it was being presented during the service. A bitter controversy arose over having the congregation learn to read notes and correctly sing the melody. The controversy was eventually resolved in a manner pleasing to the clergy: Singing Societies came into being.

Singing Societies, of course, wanted better singing. They were slowly founded all over New England to further this desire. Methods of singing and elementary music theory were taught. In many cases, the first row of seats in the gallery of the church was reserved for the best singers. These singers led the singing during the services. From these "first row" singers, church choirs evolved. The Precentors, however, were not eliminated without some bitter fights. And even today, the practice of "lining out" hymns exists in many churches as a sort of prelude beginning of the service.

With the appearance of *The Bay Psalm Hymn Book* around 1692 and the *Watts Hymnal* published in 1711, hymn music became more pleasing and the quality of the hymns improved. Hymns and hymn books continued to change, and most denominations have published several hymn books reflecting their own congregation's philosophy and needs.

### RECALL

1. The _____ came to America around 1630.
2. They brought with them a different hymn book, "The _____ _____ Book."
3. The "_____ _____ _____ _____" was the first book to be printed in the colonies.
4. The early editions of the "Whole Booke of Psalmes" contained no _____.
5. The Puritans' music used a quick and lively _____.
6. The religious denomination of the Puritans was congregational. To train their future leaders they founded the first college in America: _____ College, in 1636.
7. In England, the Parish clerk had the task of being the _____.
8. In New England, this job was given to the _____.
9. The clergy saw a need for _____ _____.

10. In many cases, the first row of seats in the gallery was reserved for the _____ _____.
11. From these "first row" singers, _____ _____ evolved.

## THE AFRICANS

The first Africans who came as New Arrivals to America were indentured servants and, like other indentured servants, were able to work for their freedom. About the middle of the seventeenth century, this changed and Africans were no longer classed as indentured servants and their right to work for freedom was lost. African New Arrivals to America during the middle 1700's were slaves.

The slaves were brought from the Ivory Coast, Liberia, Togo, Cameroon Gabon, Senegal, Gambia, Dahomey, Guinea, Sierra Leone and some parts of the Republic of the Congo. In Africa, almost all events and customs were observed with music and dancing. This included births, deaths, marriages, work and celebrations. The past and present cultural traditions and tribal history were passed along through these songs and dances.

The African societies from which the slaves were taken were both formally and informally organized. The formally organized societies had Rulers, such as Kings, Noblemen and Governors. The informally organized societies had tribes, clans and kinship groups. Virtually all of these groups spoke different languages.

The musical instruments of the Africans may be divided into four catagories:

African Call horn

1. *Aerophones* — Instruments with closed bodies through which vibrations are carried on a column of air. Examples: trumpets (usually constructed from

ivory or wood), or horns (usually constructed from tusks of elephants). The trumpet, trombone, french horn and other cup mouthpiece instruments owe their beginnings to the African Call Horns.

2. *Chordophones* — **Instruments with vibrating strings that produce sound. These include the Korro** (eighteen string harp), the Simbing (seven string harp) and the Koonting (three stringed instrument). Other chordophones (string instruments) **were the Akam, Wambee, or Valga. Akam is a** plucked string with a box-like sounding board. A varying number of canes are bound to its back with their tops extending upward and forward. Fiber strings are stretched from these canes to the base of the sound box.

3. *Membranophones* — Instruments with vibrating drum heads. Membranes are skins stretched across **hollowed bodies of various shapes. They were struck** with hands or beaters. One African Drum was the Agwel. It is a bottle-shaped, hand-played drum from Morocco.

4. *Idiophones* — Instruments which produce their sound by shaking or striking. The rattle is a familiar example of an idiophone.

The music of the Africans had the following general characteristics:

1. Syncopation — rhythm with stresses on the unaccented metric beat.

2. Pentatonic Scale — A scale of five notes to the octave. Used by many folk cultures including Africa, China, Japan, Ireland and Scotland.

(A pentatonic scale can be played by using only black keys of the piano).

3. Polyrhythm—more than one rhythm played at the same time.

4. Gap Scales

## AMERICAN SLAVE MUSIC

The enslaved Africans arriving in America late in the seventeenth century brought several musical elements: syncopation, poly-rhythm, pentatonic and gap scales and a combination of music and body movements.

They crossed the Atlantic chained in quarters too small to sit or turn around; shackled by their necks and legs to the ships's deck; fighting stench, suffocation, dysentary and hunger. Those who survived found a common language in music to tell their story. They could not talk to each other because they had been taken from many tribes with many different languages. Neither could they talk to those who owned them.

The slaves created a music which revealed their unhappiness and suffering, taught facts, sent messages, proved a common language, and shared religious rituals and beliefs. Thus, the "Spiritual," the Religious Folk Song of the slave, is a song in which the singer must express a personal connection with the Diety (God).

"Spirituals" fall into several categories:

1. The long phrase *Melodic Spiritual* — character-

istics: a slow to moderate tempo with a long and sustained phrase line. *Deep River* and *Nobody Knows the Trouble I've Seen* are good examples.

2. The *Call and Response Type Spiritual* — characteristics: a rapid and fiery spiritual tempo with a short phrase line. Examples are *Cert'nly Lord* and *Go Down Moses*. In this type of Spiritual the leader or lead soloist makes the opening statement and the group responds. Or the reverse, the group opens and the leader responds.

3. The short segmented *Syncopated Type Spiritual* — characteristics; a usually fast tempo with an incomplete or segmented phrase line. Extremely syncopated, often stimulating body response. Examples are *Shout All Over God's Heaven* (Heab'n) and *Little Lamb, Little Lamb*.

The "Jubilee" differs from the "Spiritual" in that the singer expresses no personal connection with the Diety but tells of some Biblical character or great Biblical event, either in narrative or descriptive terms. Examples: *Ezekiel Saw de Wheel* and *Joshua Fit de Battle of Jericho*.

The language of the Spiritual had double and triple meanings. Many of the original songs cannot be found; only a few have been preserved.

The earliest Spirituals were sung in native African tongues. The next language of the Spirituals combined the African accents with the speaking manner and accents of the slave as the slaves learned to speak English. These are now one of several English *dialects*—a speech that reflects a certain locality. Groups of slaves combined Their African language with the language of their new owners.

Symbolism used by the slaves allowed them to express thoughts among themselves which their inadequate language abilities limited. This symbolism also gave rise to a well developed language which the slave owners could not interpret. It borrowed concepts and images from both Africa and the new environment. Examples: *Chariot* — a traveling vehicle made like a sled used to transport tobacco in the Carolinas; *Ark* — a boat made like a barge used for moving along the river areas; *Home, Zion, Canaan, Paradise, Heab'n, Promist Land*, referred to the slave's African homeland; *Jerusalem* — the name of a town in South Hampton County, Virginia, where Nate Turner stayed in jail after the famous slave insurrection which he led; *Moses* — any friend of Black slave people or anyone who opposed slavery, such as White Methodist Bishop Francis Asbury, an 18th century Moses, and Harriet Tubman, a slave who led over 300 of her black brothers to freedom.

The Spiritual relects a true historical picture of the lives of slaves as told by slaves.

## RECALL

1. The first Africans who came to America were _____ _____ and were able to work toward their freedom.
2. Almost all events and customs were observed with _____ and _____.
3. Their past and present cultural traditions and tribal history were passed along through these _____ and _____.
4. The musical instruments of the Africans may be divided into _____ categories:
    1. _____    2. _____
    3. _____    4. _____
5. The slaves arriving in America from Africa late in the seventeenth century brought with them several musical elements: _____, _____, _____ and gap scales and a combination of music and _____ movements.
6. The _____ is the religious folk song of the slaves.
7. The_____ differs from the Spiritual in that the singer has no personal connection with the _____.
8. The _____ _____ were sung in native tongues.
9. The Spiritual reflects a _____ _____ _____ of the lives of the slaves.

## THE SOUTH

The colonists who were part of the development of the southern regions of the United States came largely from well-to-do families. Maryland was founded in 1634 by Cecillius Calvert. Most of the land was developed in a well-distributed manner which created plantation-type divisions with wide spacing between neighbors. The life in this area reflected the leisurely lifestyle of the wealthy English of the time. The Southern cities considered themselves pioneers in cultural musical activities. English customs were in vogue, such as the singing of madrigals after meals.

The early instruments used were the virginal and the spinet, as well as the viol, hautboy and french horn, most of which were imported.

The first performance of a Ballad Opera recorded in America was in 1735 in Charleston, South Carolina. It was *Flora* or *Hob in the Well*. From this sprung three regular theatrical seasons in Charleston. Although a dancing school took over the theatre for a few years, in 1754 the theatre was reopened for operas and plays.

In Upper Marlborough, Maryland, in 1752, the Kean and Murray Company opened a new theatre and performed *The Beggar's Opera* (1728-John Gay). This was the first time that an orchestra was used in the performance of an opera in America.

In Charleston, South Carolina, in 1762, the first musical society in America was founded. It was called "The St. Cecilia Society" and lasted until 1912. The Society engaged professional musicians to perform. An excellent pay scale was established, with most of the musicians being hired as they arrived from the old country. Music was played during and after dinner by well-trained musicians hired by the Society.

## RECALL

1. Maryland was founded in 1634 by _____ _____.
2. English customs were in vogue such as the _____ _____ _____ after meals.
3. The early instruments used were the virginal and the spinet, as well as the viol, hautboy and _____ _____, most of which were imported.
4. The first performance of a Ballad Opera in America was in 1735 in _____, _____, _____.
5. Upper Marlborough, Maryland, in 1752, was the first time an _____ was used in the performance of an opera in America.
6. In Charleston, South Carolina in 1762, the first musical society in America was founded. It was called "The _____ _____ _____".

## THE QUAKERS AND PENNSYLVANIA

Different groups settled in other areas of the colonies. The Quakers, who had come to America about 1656 as missionaries and settled along the central coast, were very opposed to all of their neighbors' religious practices and beliefs. They were especially opposed to music entertainment and were critical of those who disagreed with them.

The Quakers were persecuted, and it was not until after 1663 that persecution of the Quakers lessened and the attitudes of the colonies began to change. Ironically, it was the leadership of the Quakers that paved the way for a large group of music lovers to come to America.

In 1682, the "Glorious New World" or "The City of Brotherly Love" was founded by William Penn, a Quaker. Penn's purpose was to allow all religious groups and denominations to have a place where they could co-exist free from persecution and oppression. Swedish people had already come to Pennsylvania and in 1683, the Mennonites from Germany settled in Germantown, Pennsylvania.

In 1694 the German Pietists settled on the Wissahickon River about eight or nine miles from the Quaker City of Philadelphia. The German Pietists were mystics. They did not believe in marriage and felt that the world was coming to an end very soon. They were, however, rich in musical heritage and brought a mature secular and sacred, vocal and instrumental background with them from the small German communities across the ocean.

Johannes Kelpius, their leader, a well educated man with a great love for music, was the first musician to come to the Pennsylvania area. The Pietists used not only hymns, but musical instruments to accompany the singing of hymns.

It may be that Johannes Kelpius brought the first organ to America . . . it is known that he requested two clavichords from abroad "with additional strings."

Around 1700 the Gloria Dei Church, a Swedish church in Philadelphia, was dedicated. The Pietists (Hermits) were invited to provide the music. They used a choir and instrumental musical accompaniment. Justus Falckner, who had arrived with the first group, wanted to use organ music in the church. He felt the organ music would influence all groups from the Earliest Americans to the Quakers, help spread the teaching of language as well as customs and religion.

In 1703 Justus Falckner was the first German minister to be ordained in America. At his Ordination Service an organ was used. It is not clear whether the organ was brought over by Johannes Kelpius or whether Reverend Falckner had the organ imported. Jonas Auren was the Organist. Once again there was music provided by a choir and an instrumental ensemble which consisted of viols, oboes (hautboys), trombones and kettledrums.

Within a year's time the church gained a new member, Dr. Christopher Witt, an English physician who constructed an organ. This was the first organ to be built in in America.

## RECALL

1. The Quakers came to America about 1656 as missionaries and were strongly opposed to

_____.

2. It was the leadership of the Quakers who paved the way for a large number of groups of

_____ _____ to come to America.

3. The German Pietists were _____ in musical heritage.

4. _____ _____ was the first musician to come to the Pennsylvania area.

5. Around 1700 the Gloria Dei Church, a Swedish church in Philadelphia, was dedicated. The Pietists were invited to provide the music. They offered a _____ and _____ music accompaniment.

6. It is not clear whether Johannes Kelpius or Reverend Justus Falckner brought

_____ _____ to America.

7. Dr. Christopher Witt, an English physician built the first _____ in America.

## THE MORAVIANS

In 1741 a group of German New Arrivals called Moravians settled in Bethlehem, Pennsylvania. The Moravians were Protestants. Their history takes them back to the religious movement of John Hus. Music had always played an important role in the Moravian's life and his worship services. The Moravians' constant travels put them in contact with various European musical cultures of the Baroque Period which kept them aware of the latest musical happenings, composers and musical forms. Bethlehem was what could be called an American mission location. It was natural that it should become a music conscious settlement since Moravian missionaries traveled constantly between London (England), Saxony (Germany) and Bethlehem (Pennsylvania).

Their own religious musical heritage included a wealth of hymns, German chorales and even the use of older Gregorian chants (free meter chant of the early church service). The Moravians used hymns for most occasions, not just worship. Any activity they participated in might have a hymn created by the group and sung while the activity was underway. In fact, John Grimm compiled the first hymn collection for the Moravians.

A regular community 'Agapae' (love feast) was held on Saturday afternoons. People from all occupations attended. Food, conversation and the singing of hymns filled the afternoon. Some of the composed hymns were about motherhood, knitters, shepherds, ploughmen, washers, loggers, harvesters and threshers.

The first singing class was organized in Bethlehem in 1742. Some of the earliest choirs in America were founded by the Moravians. Singing in the choir was considered a great privilege. They were the first to incorporate music into the general school curriculum, and founded the first music schools in this country.

Special occasions such as birthdays and weddings, were marked by vocal and instrumental serenading groups. Bethlehem's famed trombone quartets became world renowned. These quartets played from the church belfry announcing deaths and also at grave sites following funeral services. The quartets also played whenever a special guest arrived. Among noted guests having been greeted by the trombone quartets at some of Bethlehem's outstanding musical events were the then President and Mrs. George Washington, Samuel Adams, Count Pulaski, Benjamin Franklin, LaFayette and Count Zinzendorf.

European works of Haydn and Mozart were imported by Immanuel Nitschmann who had traveled to Europe and was very informed of the latest European composers and their works.

The Archives at Bethlehem, Pennsylvania, exhibit manuscript copies of Haydn Quartets and nine Haydn Symphonies. Also in the collection are manuscript copies of three symphonies and six trios by Mozart dated 1785.

Bethlehem produced several composers who wrote mostly for instruments and instrumental combinations. Among the Moravian composers in Bethlehem were: (1) John Frederick Peter (1746-1813), a violinist and organist. He came to America in 1769, arriving in Bethlehem in 1770. He was reported to be the first of the Moravian composers. Although records do not indicate that Peter and Mozart ever met, they both employed unusual instrumentation in their quintets—Mozart, 1787, Peters, 1789. (2) John Antes (1740—date of death not exactly known). Antes played all of the string instruments. He was greatly influenced by Haydn and it is reported that his music sounded much like Haydn's. The names of his works are not known, but Haydn is said to have played some of his compositions. (3) David Moritz Michael (1751-1825), although born in Germany, lived for many years in Bethlehem and Nazareth (Pennsylvania).

Other Moravian composers were Brissel (Philadelphia), Dencke, Oerter and Herbst.

Orchestral instruments were used during church services in Bethlehem. These instruments included strings, oboes, flutes, horns, trumpets and kettledrums. This influence undoubtedly came from the European schools where liturgical music included instruments and sometimes the harpsichord and organ. Haydn used instrumental music scored for the church. Many composers of the eighteenth century made use of the instrumental scores in their liturgical music.

In 1744 the Collegium Musicum was organized in Bethlehem to play symphonic music. The membership was open to all who wanted to participate. The music used was sometimes published but, more often, copied by hand. Instruments were usually imported or brought over by various missionaries. Some string instruments were made by the members.

This instrumental music conscious community soon developed a symphony orchestra which grew to full instrumentation by 1761. Concerts were continuously given for over fifty years. Haydn's *Creation* was performed at Bethlehem in 1811 and Handel's *Messiah* was hand copied for its first Bethlehem performance.

A spinet piano was the first accompanying instrument used in Bethlehem in 1774. And in 1746, an organ built in Philadelphia was used. By 1791 the Moravians had established themselves as organ builders and built most of the organs for their churches which, at that time, numbered fourteen.

The largest was the organ in Zion church in Philadelphia installed in 1791. It is reported that the President and Mrs. Washington attended this service, as well as members of the Congress.

Bethlehem was a highly musical settlement where the citizens worked by day and performed music during their free time and after work. The famous Bach Festivals were started here and are still held today. Usually a choir made up of citizens along with some college choirs perform Bach's great works. It is heralded by the trombone choir which plays chorales from the church belfry.

The Moravians tended to follow the European musical traditions and they kept European music alive in America in their very active music culture. Because of this, the Moravians have received less recognition than deserved for their contributions to music in America.

THE Bethlehem Bach Choir

### RECALL

1. The Moravians settled in _____,
   _____.
2. The first _____ _____
   was organized in Bethlehem in 1742.
3. The Moravians also founded the first
   _____ _____ in this
   country.
4. Bethlehem's famed _____ quartets
   became world renowned.
5. European works of _____ and
   _____ were imported by Immanual
   Nitschmann.
6. _____ were used during church
   services in Bethlehem.
7. Haydn's "_____" was performed at
   Bethlehem in 1811 and Handel's
   "_____" was hand written for its
   first Bethlehem performance.
8. A _____ _____ was
   the first accompanying instrument used in
   Bethlehem in 1744.

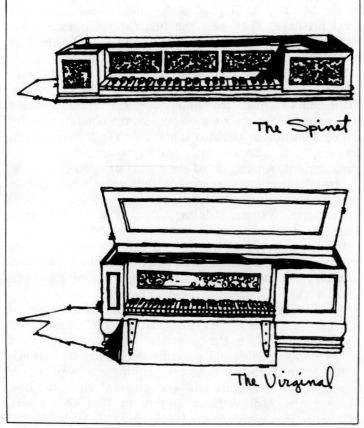

The Spinet

The Virginal

# EUROPE

# Rococo (Pre-Classical) 1725-1775

# and Classical Periods in Music 1750-1850

# EUROPE

## Rococo (Pre-Classical) 1725-1775
## and Classical Periods in Music 1750-1850

## The Rococo Period

Near the end of the Baroque Period, Bach's sons along with Domenico Scarlatti (1685-1757), an Italian composer, developed a new and interesting, although plain, musical style. The rhythms were very easy with simple harmonies. The musical form reflected a lack of proportion (irregular balance). The subject matter was mostly senseless, non-serious and often silly. Many amateurs of noble status were then able to enjoy performing music. This was known as the Rococo (or pre-classical) Period, and its music is still popular with music fans today.

With the emergence of Haydn and Mozart, clearly defined musical *forms* were established within which the classical composers usually expressed their musical ideas.

In music of the Classical Period, the following musical characteristics are dominant:

1. Instrumental music is more important than vocal music.
2. The piano is the most popular keyboard instrument.
3. The orchestra becomes standardized with four parts: strings woodwinds, brass and percussion.
4. The violin emerges as the principal orchestral instrument.
5. Melodies become more thematic.
6. Rhythms use meters which are simpler and more regular.
7. Music uses several key contrasts.
8. The highest voice usually carries the melody while the lower voices provide the harmony and bass.
9. Cadences are frequent.

Some musical forms of the Classical Period—

Instrumental: Sonata—Allegro, Sonatina, Sonata, Concerto, Symphony, string trio, string quartet, divertimento
Vocal: Mass

## The Classical Period
### THE ERA OF PERFECTING MUSICAL FORMS

Important American events during the Classical Period:

Two Wars—
The French and Indian War (1756-1763).
The War of 1812 (United States and England).
Important Discoveries—
The invention of Isaac Watts' steam engine (1765).
The invention of Robert Fulton's steam boat (1808).
The invention of the cotton gin by Eli Whitney (1793).

The adoption of the United States Declaration of Independence (1776).
The signing of the Bill of Rights (1791).
The opening of the Erie Canal (1825).
The Louisiana Purchase (1803).

### FRANZ JOSEPH HAYDN
### 1732-1803

Franz Joseph Haydn brought instrumental music of the Classical Period to great heights during his lifetime. Vocal music had already enjoyed a very high status.

Haydn was born in Rohrau, Austria, to a poor but deeply religious family; his father was a wheelwright and his

Haydn

mother, a cook. Haydn was the second child born to this couple who had a total of twelve children.

Joseph's musical ability was evident when he was five years old. A cousin took charge of his musical training and took Haydn to Hainburg with him.

At an early age, Haydn became a member of the choir of St. Stephen's Cathedral in Vienna, Austria. When Haydn was fifteen, Maria Theresa (the Empress) noticed Haydn's voice change and commented, "Young Haydn's singing is like unto the crowing of a cock." Haydn was subsequently dismissed and left with no means of support.

Haydn studied the harpsichord and violin and also had an excellent foundation in vocal techniques. However, for the next six years Haydn did odd jobs, taught a few pupils, played the violin as often as possible for pay and purchased and studied as many musical manuscripts as he could obtain. Among those musical scores were some by Carl Philip Emanual Bach (J.S. Bach's son).

Haydn became the accompanist and valet for Nicola Porpora (1686-1766), an Italian composer, theorist and vocal teacher, in exchange for his musical studies. During this six year period Haydn wrote his first Mass, his first string quartet and a comic opera (for which the music has been lost).

Haydn's contact with Porpora placed him in the presence of many noble and wealthy people. It was through a wealthy friend, Von Funberg, that Haydn was appointed to the position as music director to Count Morzin in 1759. Here he wrote his first symphony, following basically the sonata form of C.P.E. Bach. Haydn had been greatly influenced in his symphony writing by this sonata form and by the writings of C.P.E. Bach. However, it was Haydn's string quartet which brought him recognition by the nobility and the upper class.

The Count was influenced by the Countess to send Haydn many financially able students and to allow Haydn to conduct the Count's private orchestra. When the orchestra was dismissed in 1761, Prince Paul A. Esterhazy of Eisenstadt, Hungary, immediately hired Haydn as his assistant choir master. When Prince Michael Esterhazy succeeded his brother Paul in 1766, Haydn became the conductor of the orchestra, acclaimed as the best private orchestra in the world at that time. Haydn worked for the Esterhazy family for over thirty years and wrote most of his major works in the Esterhazy employ.

Haydn composed a symphony for Maria Theresa, the Empress of Austria, and a frequent visitor to the Esterhazy court. The symphony was called the *Maria Theresa Symphony*. (How ironic, because this was the same lady who had caused him to lose his singing job in Vienna when fifteen years old!)

When Haydn visited the city of Bonn, he met young Ludwig van Beethoven who became one of his students. Beethoven was a low-paying student and very self assured. The pupil-teacher relationship between the two became strained, and Haydn and Beethoven did not get along well. Haydn referred to Beethoven as "The Great Mongol," and spent as little time as possible with the promising student.

Unlike the relationship between Haydn and Beethoven, Haydn's other famous student, Mozart, shared a kindred feeling with his master-teacher. Haydn's own symphonic style and form were influenced by Mozart. George P. Bridgetower, an outstanding violinist-composer of the time, was also a student of Franz Joseph Haydn.

Haydn developed several forms or models for the "string quartet" which he finally established as a significant musical group with its own repertory. He also enriched and further developed the "sonata" form, the major pattern used for some of the movements in the larger "symphony" form.

Haydn divided his orchestra into sections: string, woodwind, brass and percussion, thus standardizing the orchestra as we know it today. He added the "Minuet" as a third movement to the "symphony" form, thus establishing the now common four movement symphony.

"Papa Haydn", as he was respectfully called, was not a pianist, but he did compose over fifty piano sonatas. His music is delicate, spirited and well balanced with a feeling of optimism, delight, love and hope. Haydn's themes touch all people of all ages in a clear but simple and refreshing manner. Haydn is called the Father of the Modern Symphony Orchestra.

Haydn's works number over a thousand and include symphonies, string quartets, trios, operas, sonatas, Masses, motets (his famous *Last Words of Christ*), songs, airs and cannons, works for the stage, and pieces for the baryton, (a string instrument with a bow, played by Prince Esterhazy, which was obsolete by the 19th century).

## RECALL

1. Franz Joseph Haydn brought _____ music to great heights during his lifetime.
2. Haydn studied the _____ and _____ and also had an excellent foundation in vocal technique.
3. Haydn became an accompanist and valet for Nicola Porpora. During this period, he wrote his first _____ and his first _____ _____.
4. When Prince Michael Esterhazy succeeded his brother Paul in 1766, Haydn became the _____ of the _____.
5. When Haydn visited the city of Bonn, he met the young _____ who became one of his students.
6. _____ was also a student of Haydn's.
7. Haydn divided the symphony orchestra into sections, thus _____ the symphony.

## WOLFGANG AMADEUS MOZART
## 1756-1791

Wolfgang Amadeus Mozart, the child performer and composer, was one of the world's greatest musical genuises. He was born in Salzburg, Austria. When he was three years old he played little compositions on the keyboard. By the age of six he was able to sightread and play music on the violin which many other people had to practice. At seven, Mozart conducted one of his own orchestra compositions. By the time he was ten, he was able to play the organ, violin and clavier as well as almost any professional musician.

His original compositions at the age of ten included piano sonatas, two Italian arias, a full symphony, and the first part of an oratorio; by twelve, he had written an opera and a comic opera and by fourteen, a grand opera.

Mozart once heard a *Miserere* by the Italian priest and composer Gregorio Allegri (1582-1652) sung by the Sistine Choir in Rome. When he went home he wrote out the complete *Miserere* as he had heard it.

Mozart began traveling on concert tours with his sister, Maria Anna (nicknamed "Nannerl"), when he was seven years old. These tours lasted until Mozart was fifteen.

Leopold Mozart, Wolfgang and Nannerl's father, was a composer and violinist who worked for the Archbishop of Salzburg. Leopold Mozart arranged the tours for his children and trained and developed their musical talents. He felt traveling was an important aspect of excellent musical training and also hoped to expose Mozart's genius to nobility so that he would (when he became an adult) be able to obtain a high paying Court appointment.

Some of the great cities the Mozarts traveled to included Leipzig, Rome, Paris, and cities of Austria, Switzerland and England. During these tours Mozart met Haydn and studied with him. Mozart had a great influence on Haydn and both Mozart and Haydn developed the classic symphony.

The "Haydn Quartets", six string quartets written by Mozart, publicly displayed Mozart's gratitude to the master composer.

Mozart's father continually tried to obtain a high Court position in Vienna for his son, but this dream never materialized. Thus, Wolfgang had to resort to giving lessons and performing on programs and in concerts until he died. Frequently in financial trouble, Mozart died a very poor man and was buried in a public cemetary with no grave marker.

Mozart gave opera a new status and developed it to its fullest. The *Magic Flute* and *Don Giovanni* are two of the most popular performed by most modern opera companies. He highlighted and made use of the clarinet in the symphony and added the trombone to the symphony orchestra. He also brought a fuller, more developed form to the piano concerto to which other composers would add personal variations.

The last work Mozart composed was his *Requiem* (A Mass for the Dead). Mozart became very ill while writing this work, but continued to write the music. According to his wife and friends, he believed he was writing this work for his own funeral. When Mozart died in 1791, his *Requiem* was completely sketched, but unfinished. A very personal friend, Lanz Xaver Sussmayr (1766-1803), completed the orchestral score from the sketch which Mozart had laid out. Mozart left the world the great gift of his music and was one of the few composers who wrote in every area of music including 18 operas, 40 symphonies, 13 masses, 26 quartets, and many concertos, choral works and other instrumental music.

## RECALL

1. By the time Mozart was ten, he was able to play the _____,
_____ and _____.
2. Mozart had a great influence on _____.
3. He gave _____ a new status and developed it to its fullest.
4. Mozart died a _____ and was buried in a public cemetary with no grave marker.
5. Mozart's last work was his "_____".

# LUDWIG VAN BEETHOVEN
# 1770-1827

To a woman who worked as a cook and a man who was a professional singer, but drank too much, was born one of the greatest musicians of all times, Ludwig van Beethoven. When he was born, his family was living in Bonn, Germany, where his father was a chapel singer hired by the Archbishop Elector of Bonn.

Beethoven's father was often very cruel to him, yet was his first teacher. He required him to practice long hours. It was his mother who protected him from heavy abuse by his father.

At the age of four, Beethoven could play the clavier. By eight, he could play the violin. By the time he was thirteen, he played the cembalo (harpsichord) at a theatre and was able to conduct and compose.

After becoming a student of the Court organist, Christian Gottlob Neefe (1748-1798), Beethoven's musical concepts and knowledge grew. He soon became Neefe's assistant and earned his first pay in music.

By 1783 he was recognized for his compositional ability and was brought to the attention of Mozart. In 1787 Mozart heard Beethoven play and stated that "young Beethoven will make a noise in the world." That same year (1787) Beethoven's mother and sister died and this left him to suffer the unbearable meaness of his drunken father. The courts alloted Beethoven part of his father's salary in

Ludwig
Van Beethoven

1789. A home was provided for him by a widow, the mother of two of his students. He also met Count Waldstein who became a friend for life and a patron of Beethoven. In 1792 Beethoven was sent to Vienna by the Elector where he studied with the great master, Haydn, for two years. They did not get on well. The Society of Vienna recognized Beethoven's ability even though his teachers thought him too uncultured in manner and too free with his musical ideas. Beethoven was very organized and kept a notebook so he could write his musical ideas whenever they occurred. Because of his very frank, blunt mannerisms, Beethoven was thought to be temperamental.

In spite of this, his great musical ability gained respect for him from many noble personages who constantly sought his company.

Most musicians of the time were classified almost as servants, but Beethoven would not accept this status and was treated on an equal basis with his noble friends. Very few people wanted to alienate him.

Beethoven was a pianist of magnificent ability with no equal. His compostions can be divided into three periods. **The First Period**—1792-1802: His works during this period reflect the classic structure used by Haydn and Mozart. Some authors refer to this period as "The Period of Imitation" or "Assimilation." Although Beethoven followed the classic form, his innovative ideas are evident. The fixed order of the sonata form in terms of movements which had become traditional did not constrict him. He allowed his ideas to dictate the order of the movements. He wrote thirty eight piano sonatas, two symphonies and three piano concertos during this period.

**The Second Period**—1802-1815: Beethoven now began to have problems with his hearing. His loss of hearing started around 1800 stemming from a bad case of typhoid fever when he was young which caused the acoustic nerve to degenerate. In addition to this problem, these years were also full of domestic unrest. He had to contend with two brothers and a nephew who did not appreciate and were not grateful for the assistance he provided for them.

He was also continuously agitated by the frequent times he had to move and the difficulty he had in keeping servants. These conditions along with his hearing loss caused Beethoven to be very irritable and often unnecessarily suspicious of many of his friends. He wrote his opera *Fidelio* and the *Eroica Symphony* during this period.

Beethoven believed in the principles of democracy and he was happy to dedicate his symphony, the *Eroica*, to Napoleon because he felt he represented those principles. However, when it was revealed that Napoleon had himself elected Emperor, Beethoven went into a rage and destroyed the first page and changed the name of his symphony.

**The Third Period**—1815-1827: Beethoven was, by this time, completely deaf. Yet, during this period, he wrote his famed *Ninth Symphony* and his *Mass in D*. He also wrote many of his piano sonatas.

When composing, Beethoven became completely absorbed in his creativity. He was totally unaware of his surroundings and had absolutely no concern for his personal needs. He wrote his ideas several times before becoming satisfied with the final idea.

Beethoven was the first composer to earn his living from music. His life and work span the end of the period called "Classical" and the beginning of the period called "Romantic."

### RECALL

1. Beethoven's _____ was his first teacher.
2. By 1783 Beethoven was recognized for his compositional ability and was brought to the attention of _____.
3. Beethoven studied with the great master _____.
4. Beethoven was a _____ of magnificent ability.

5. During his Second Period, he wrote his opera "_____" and the "_____ _____."
6. During his Third Period, although completely deaf, he wrote his famed "_____ _____".
7. Beethoven was the first composer to earn a _____ from music.

## GEORGE P. BRIDGETOWER
## 1779-1860

George P. Bridgetower was born on February 29, 1779, in Viola, Poland, of an African father and a Polish mother. His family was considered of the upper class.

Bridgetower's parents soon noticed his unusual musical talent and they secured some of the finest teachers available Among his teachers were Haydn and Bartholomew. George became a masterful, skillful violinist and gave his first concert when he was ten. He later became the violinist for the Prince of Wales at Brighton.

Many people saw the need for the talented Bridgetower to meet the great master Beethoven. Such a meeting was arranged and they quickly became close friends. Beethoven became a Bridgetower admirer and they began to concertize together.

Bridgetower, also known as the "Abyssinian Prince," was an excellent composer and wrote over forty pianoforte suites. The *Henry* ballad was dedicated to the Princess Royal in London. Many of Bridgetower's works are lost and *Henry* is the only ballad remaining.

The *Kreutzer Sonata* by Beethoven was written especially for Bridgetower. George P. Bridgetower traveled on concert tours to many countries and died at 81 years of age.

### RECALL

1. Among Bridgetower's teachers were _____ and _____.
2. He became the _____ for the Prince of Wales at Brighton.
3. _____ became a Bridgetower admirer and they began to concertize together.
4. Many of Bridgetower's works are lost and "_____" is the only ballad remaining.

# AMERICA
# 1725-1825

# AMERICA 1725-1825

## FRANCIS HOPKINSON
## 1737-1791

Francis Hopkinson was one of the signers of the Declaration of Independence and the first Secretary of the United States Navy. He was also a lawyer and a graduate of the College of Philadelphia, now known as the University of Philadelphia.

Chamber music (small instrumental groups) was often performed in Hopkinson's early Philadelphia. Concerts were given and the music played varied from Pergolesi and Scarlatti to Handel, Arnes and Purcell. Hopkinson played church services, taught singing (he was a Psalmodist—one who arranges songs for singing) and began his musical career at the age of seventeen. In addition, Hopkinson was a writer, painter and inventor.

He was an authority on rhythm and phrasing and was constantly requesting "dignity" in the music for the church.

He also desired that the chanting used in the church be phrased rhythmically to express the phrase and the thought.

Among his musical works is a collection of *Seven Songs for the Harpsichord* (first presented to the public in 1788). Also written was a book of songs containing *My Days Have Been So Wondrous Free*, several secular songs and religious compositions (the 114th Psalm and the 23rd Psalm) and probably a collection of Psalms and anthems for two churches in Philadelphia.

Francis Hopkinson dedicated his collection of harpsichord numbers called *Seven Songs for the Harpsichord or Forte Piano* to his friend George Washington, who was not yet president. Another of his works dedicated to George Washington, entitled *A Toast*, was written during the Revolutionary War. The first American music publisher published this work, words and music, in 1799, 21 years after it was written.

*The Temple of Minerva*, a dramatic cantata/opera type, was also one of Francis Hopkinson's major compositions.

Although musical scripts of this work have not been found, there is indication that a performance was given in Philadelphia on December 19, 1781 with George Washington in the audience. This would then have been America's first performance of a dramatic cantata/opera type composed by a native composer. In the early 1930's, many works of this first native American composer appeared. These manuscripts were suspected of being false and when checked by experts, it was revealed that a single individual (a forger) was responsible for them. However one of the books which was traced back to ownership by the first United States Treasurer, Michael Hillegas (1729-1804), is legitimate. Other works by Francis Hopkinson can be found in the Library of Congress.

Hopkinson invented a new device for quilling harpsichords and improved the harmonica. His works, unfortunately, had no influence on later American composers. They do, however show the existence of structured music in the colonies (F. Hopkinson's *Ode on Music*-1754) and reveal that structured music had a place in our early American society.

Francis Hopkinson's musical training is difficult to trace. There was a constant influx of musicians from Europe to America. One of Hopkinson's compositions, *An Ode to the Memory of James Bremner*, indicates that he studied with James Bremner who was a noted musician in Philadelphia, having arrived around 1762.

Francis Hopkinson's songs are almost the only record we have of any early American composers of structured secular song—1759. Only a few of his songs are available. The Library of Congress has a record of them: *The Garland, My Days Have Been So Wondrous Free, and Oh! Come to Mason Borough's Grove*. Most of them were written in two parts, treble voices and bass voices, with the indicated harmonies then used by the harpsichord player.

## RECALL

1. Francis Hopkinson was one of the signers of the _____ _____ _____ and the first Secretary of the _____.
2. Hopkinson played for church services, taught _____ and began his musical career at the age of seventeen.
3. He was an authority on _____ and phrasing.
4. Hopkinson dedicated several of his works to his friend, _____ _____.
5. "The _____ _____ _____" may have been America's first performance of a dramatic cantata/opera by a native composer.
6. Francis Hopkinson's songs are almost the only record we have of any early American Composers of _____ secular song.

## JAMES LYON
### 1735-1794

A contemporary of Francis Hopkinson was James Lyon, a Presbyterian minister who was equally interested in music and the ministry. During his college days he revealed his ability to compose. For one commencement program at the College of New Jersey (later Princeton) in 1761 he shared the program with his contemporary, Francis Hopkinson. James Lyon composed an anthem which was used and later, that same afternoon, Francis Hopkinson's composition, *An Ode*, was performed. After becoming a Presbyterian minister, James Lyon went to Nova Scotia and, during the revolution, was willing to lead a campaign to conquer this territory. He even wrote to George Washington and requested permission to do this. Because of the meager salary given him in Nova Scotia, he later had to return to Maine.

Lyon's most noted work, called *Urania* or *A Choice Collection of Psalm-tunes, Anthems and Hymns*, was written during his stay in Philadelphia. Included were six entirely new works written for two, three and four part singing. *Urania* was dedicated to all ministers of all denominations and sold several editions.

*God Save the King*, published in 1761, made its first appearance in America in this book. This is the tune we now call *America*. The Colonists simply changed the words in various ways including "God Save George Washington" and "God save the 13 states." Lyon used the words "Come Thou Almight King," *Urania*, and it was called Whitefield's tune. The words that we sing to "America" today were written by Samuel Francis Smith in 1832, a young minister. Smith was not aware at the time that he was writing words for our first National Anthem which were destined to become famous.

James Lyon wrote many other tunes during his stay in Maine, most, if not all of them unpublished. Of the few songs from the early days which survived, *Mear*, the first tune in Lyon's book, can still be found in several old hymn books. Two composers are given credit for writing it: one English by the name of John Barnard who published a Psalm book in 1727, and an American also with the name of John Barnard, a minister in Massachusetts who is supposed to have composed this song in 1727. If true , *Mear* would be a song sung in early American and still surviving, and John Barnard would be the first American composer of whom we still have musical knowledge and manuscripts.

## RECALL

1. James Lyon was a Presbyterian minister equally interested in _____ and the ministry.

2. For one commencement program at the College of Pennsylvania in 1761, he shared the program with his contemporary _____ _____.

3. "God Save The King" is also called "_____".

## WILLIAM BILLINGS
### 1746-1800

William Billings was born in Boston and became very active in developing church choirs and Singing Societies. The singing interest in New England had lessened between 1720 and 1820 and it was the musical interest and efforts of Billings which revived the singing enthusiasm of the New England people.

Billings introduced the use of the pitch pipe for church services. This soon improved the singing of the congregation which usually suffered from pitch difficulties. Billings also made use of the violoncello in the church service which was a startling innovation for the day.

William Billings was an exciting composer. He owned a leather tannery but spent much of his time writing out his musical ideas, even during business hours. He had very little formal musical training and read from a musical treatise to gain what musical insight he acquired. Billings was a self-taught composer-musician who broke away from the typical pattern of Psalm tunes and hymns to create what he called "Fuguing Pieces." "Fuguing Pieces," an imitative counterpoint style, were really attempts by Billings to have the congregation sing more powerful tunes with each section mastering its own part.

Billings' "Fuguing Pieces" have been referred to as not fugues at all, but attempts at fugues because he lacked the trained technique and sufficient musical training necessary to enhance his ideas . However, Billings' works reflect genuine creative thoughts and put a musical vitality into our country's early music. His music was more popular than the music of European composers in America during those days. Almost every Psalm book of that time contained some music by Billings.

Today, there has been a revival and a new interest in Billings' works. Many of his compositions have been published along with new arrangements by modern day writers. Billings' most famous work, *Chester* is still very popular today. Both vocal and instrumental writers — sacred and secular — make use of this powerful, vigorous piece. Billings published two books, *The New England Psalm Singer* which he called "Reuben" and *The Singing Master's Assistant* which was finally known as "Billings' Best."

His first book was criticized for using too many simple tunes and making no use of dissonance. This caused him to revise many of the tunes.

His composition *Jargon* included dissonance and is considered one of the first American modern compositons much on the order of the music of Schoenberg and Stravinsky. Dissonance prevailed throughout and, accompanying the piece, Billings included a manifesto to the Goddess of Discord. His other works included *Over There* (new words to the song *Chester* used during the Revolution) and *Lamentation Over Boston* (in which he paraphrased the words from the Bible and changed the locale in Psalm 137 to mean Boston when the British troops occupied it). His other published collections were *The Psalm Singer's Amusement, The Suffolk Harmony, The Continental Harmony* and *Music in Miniature*.

Billings was married and had six children. He was continually in financial need. Physically, he would be described as having a withered arm, one leg shorter than the other, a rather gruff voice and blind in one eye. The blessings of the music that he wrote poured from his inner beauty and the need for a new musical expression in his day.

## RECALL

1. William Billings became very active in developing _____ _____ and Singing Societies.
2. He introduced the use of the _____ _____ for church services.
3. He had very little _____ musical training.

4. Billings' music was more _____ than the music of European composers in America during that day.
5. Billings' composition "*Jargon*" included _____ and is considered one of the first American modern compositions.
6. Name Billings' most famous work:
_____.

## SINGING FAMILIES

Beginning in 1800, the Singing Families of America made their songs the popular songs of America. Any group of four was called a Family and usually included two women and two men.

The music performed ranged from original short works to ballads covering the full range of life, including nonsense and make-believe. The harmony was simple and the Singing Family improvised. The style called for well blended voices—with closed harmony.

One outstanding Family was the Hutchinson Family from New Hampshire. They were for temperance (no alcohol) and revival (religious rededication) and used their singing travels to promote their points of view on social conditions of the day. Their programs included over a dozen anti-slavery songs, revival songs and temperance songs.

Another Singing Family was the Rainer Family. They had a rich musical heritage coming from their life in the mountains which they carried world-wide in singing their songs.

### RECALL

1. Beginning in 1800 the _____ _____ of America made their songs the popular songs of America.
2. Any group of _____ was called a Family.
3. These Families usually traveled _____-_____ singing their songs.

The Hutchinson Family

## THE HYMN—AMERICAN GOSPEL (WHITE)

About 1800 in America the great religious revival began. The revival represented a period in American music during which the traveling preacher (Evangelist) stirred his audience to religious rededication, not only with his sermons, but also with his music.

Many preachers wrote their own hymns. At the beginning, the words were printed and passed out in pamphlet form. However, shape note hymnals soon began to appear with words and music. The interest in singing these new songs then increased. The revival movement was largely Protestant and it swept the country. Such names as

Dwight L. Moody, Ira D. Sankey (1804-1908), Isaac Watts (1674-1748), P.P. Bliss (1838-1876), George C. Stebbins (1846-1945), Fanny Crosby (1820-1915), W.H. Doane (1832-1915), George F. Root (1820-1895), Rev. Charles Wesley (1707-1788), C.C. Converse (1832-1918), Ray Palmer (1808-1887), and Lowell Mason (1792-1872), are but a few of the hymn writers of that era.

The hymns they wrote were called Gospel hymns. Gospel hymns were generally thought of by music historians as contributing very little to American musical literature. They were simply songs used in Protestant churches and lacked the restraint that earlier hymns and chorales possessed. Many of the tunes which were used in Gospel hymns carried traces of earlier folk tunes that had been handed down through the years. But, many also were original. Over 600 songs can be easily credited to this period.

Some of these songs still may be heard in today's religious services. They continue to stir the emotions and enhance the services. This effect is largely due to the popular style melody which these hymns reflect. This type of melody allows for an additional input, when desired, on the part of the performer (singer and/or accompanist) which can "decorate" the performance of the hymn. This, perhaps accounts for the title, Gospel, where the hymn by itself is a small sermonette in song (a telling of the Gospel through song ).

Here are some hymns now used in many Protestant and Catholic churches, neither of which at one time would have recognized any Gospel hymn.

"I Need Thee Every Hour"
   Mrs. Annie S. Hawks — Rev. Robert Lowry
"The Ninety and Nine"
   Elizabeth C. Clephane — Ira D. Sankey
"I Am Praying For You"
   S. O'Maley Cluff — Ira D. Sankey
"Rescue The Perishing"
   Fanny J. Crosby — W. H. Doane
"What Hast Thou Done For Me?"
   Frances R. Havergal — P.P. Bliss
"Pass Me Not"
   Fanny J. Crosby — W.H. Doane
"What A Friend We Have In Jesus"
   Charles C. Converse
"I Love To Tell The Story"
   Kate Hankey — W.G. Fischer
"Sweet Hour Of Prayer"
   Rev. W.W. Walford — Wm. B. Bradbury
"Jesus, Lover Of My Soul"
   Rev. C. Wesley — Simeon B. Marsh
"Rock Of Ages"
   Rev. A. M. Toplady — Dr. Thomas Hastings
"Yield Not To Temptation"
   H.R. Palmer
"Onward Christian Soldiers"
   Rev. S. Baring-Gould — Dr. Thomas Hastings
"Come Ye Disconsolate"
   Thomas Moore & Thomas Hastings — Samuel Webbe
"It is Well With My Soul"
   H.G. Stafford — P.P. Bliss
"Holy, Holy! Lord God Almighty"
   Reginald Heber, D.D. — Rev. John B. Dykes
"Bringing In The Sheaves"
   Knowles Shaw — George A. Minor
"When I Survey The Wondrous Cross"
   Isaac Watts — Ed. by Lowell Mason
"Peace Be Still"
   Miss M. A. Baker — H.R. Palmer
"The Precious Name"
   Mrs. Lydia Baxter — W.H. Doane
"Nearer My God To Thee"
   Bethany — Lowell Mason
"My Faith Looks Up To Thee"
   Olivet — Lowell Mason
"Stand Up, Stand Up For Jesus"
   George James Webb

"He Leadeth Me"
   Joseph Gilmore
"Just As I Am, Without One Plea"
   Charlotte Elliott
"Savior Like A Shepherd Lead Me"
   Dorothy Thrupp
"Sweet Hour Of Prayer"
   William Walford

## RECALL

1. About 1800 in America the great
   _____ _____ began.
2. Many _____ wrote their own hymns.
3. Name three hymn writers of this era:
   _____, _____ and
   _____.
4. The hymns they wrote were called
   _____ hymns.
5. In Gospel, the hymn itself is a small sermonette in _____.

## LOWELL MASON
## 1792-1872

A history of American music would not be complete without Lowell Mason. He is known as the Father of

Lowell Mason

American Music Education. Lowell Mason is credited with beginning the movement that was to set the stage for the large scale involvement with music that each American enjoys today.

Mason was born in Medfield, Massachusetts, and played several musical instruments including the organ and piano. Although comfortably established as an organist and choir director, Mason firmly believed that elementary school children had the right to a musical education. He was influenced by the Pestalonian methods of teaching which were contemporary methods used in Europe. He experimented with and developed curriculum and methods of teaching singing to children.

In the beginning, children in the Boston area were invitied to participate in Mason's new music program free of charge if they would remain for at least one year. The singing program was a big success. The classes were first held in a church. Mason then turned his energy to convincing Boards of Education that young children needed education in music as well as in the traditional subjects. This was a new concept and it is surprising that Mason finally succeeded.

He gave many public concerts with his young students, which not only proved his theory about teaching singing, but also demonstrated their ability to artistically express themselves through music. His public concerts led to the establishment of the Boston Academy of Music.

After a series of successful concerts by students of the Boston Academy of Music, Lowell Mason was appointed to be the very first Superintendent of Public School Music on August 28, 1837. The next year, the Boston Board of Education appropriated money for public school music education; but, it forgot to authorize money for music teachers and Mason's salary.

Lowell Mason's important accomplishments may be summed up as follows:

1. He established a place for vocal music in the schools.
2. He sponsored training conventions for public school music teachers.
3. He edited and revised several hymns and hymn books, published popular collections of music for

home and choir and is the composer of two of our best known hymns, *Nearer My God To Thee* and *My Faith Looks Up To Thee.*
4. He made music education for the masses of American students a reality.
5. He replaced the traveling music teachers at that time with permanently resident music teachers.

## RECALL

1. _____ _____ is known as the "Father of American Music Education."
2. Although comfortably established as an _____ and _____, Mason firmly believed that elementary school children should have the right to a musical education.
3. He was influenced by the _____ methods of teaching which were contemporary methods used in Europe.
4. His public concerts led to the establishment of the _____ _____ of _____.
5. Lowel Mason was appointed to be the very first _____ of Public School Music.
6. He is the composer of two of our best known hymns: "_____ _____ _____ _____ _____" and "_____ _____ _____ _____ _____".

# EUROPE

# Romantic and Impressionistic Periods

# EUROPE
## ROMANTIC AND IMPRESSIONISTIC PERIODS

## The Romantic Period in Music
## 1825-1900

This era was one of personal emotional expression by artists. It was part of the new-found freedom which ended the class system and allowed a man to be whatever his abilities and drive would permit. Self-expression with vivid descriptiveness became the goal.

Some musical characteristics of the Romantic Period are:
1. Opera houses, concert halls and salons became the performing places for artists.
2. A decline of interest in church music.
3. The performer shows his skill and ability to master instruments when performing.
4. The symphony orchestra is enlarged and the English horn, trombone, tuba, harp, piano and many new percussion instruments are added.
5. The piano is used to accompany the vocal soloists.
6. Melody lines make use of chromatic movement with opposite contour.
7. Harmony becomes rich in dissonance which adds to the emotional tension desired.
8. There is much use of free imitation (repetition) with melodies.
9. Modulation (changing of key) is frequent.
10. Rhythm becomes much more flexible with meter changes, syncopation and flexible rubato (speed changes according to emotion).

Some representative musical forms from the Romantic Period are—

Instrumental: Character piece, concert overture, tone poem, rhapsody

Vocal: the Art Song (Lieder)

## Romantic Period in History

Events occuring during this Period were:

Three important Inventions—
  The telegraph by Samuel Morse (1832).
  The telephone by Alexander Graham Bell (1876).
  The phonograph by Thomas Edison (1877).

and—
  The American Civil War (1861-1865).
  The Emancipation Proclamation (1863).
  The Assassination of Abraham Lincoln (1865).
  The dedication of the Statue of Liberty (1886).
  Radium discovered by Marie and Pierre Curie (1898).

## The Waltz Kings

### JOHANN STRAUSS, SR.
### 1804-1889

Johann Strauss, the father of Johann Strauss Jr., had parents who did not want him to become a professional musician. However, by the time he was fifteen, he was performing with a group in Vienna, Austria and eventually became the leader. Strauss Sr. developed a successful music business in Vienna, and had several musicians working for him. He wrote about one hundred and fifty waltzes.

### JOHANN STRAUSS, JR.
### 1825-1899

Johann Strauss, the son, surprisingly did not have his father's encouragement when he himself wanted to become a composer. Nevertheless, when he was six, he wrote his first waltz. By the time he was nineteen, he had made an appearance as a guest conductor for an orchestra.

It was not until after the senior Strauss' death that the younger Strauss formed his own orchestra. This orchestra eventually traveled all over the world including America.

Johann Strauss became a prolific writer (over four hundred waltzes) and was noted for his operas, *Die Fledermaus* and *The Gypsy Baron*. *The Blue Danube* and *Tales of the Vienna Woods* are two of his most popular waltzes.

Johann
Strauss Jr.

## RECALL

1. Johann Strauss' parents did _____ want him to become a professional musician.
2. He wrote about _____ waltzes.
3. After his father's death, Johann Strauss (the son) formed an _____.
4. Johann Strauss Junior's most famous waltzes are "_____ _____" and "_____ _____ _____ _____ _____".

## FRANZ SCHUBERT
### 1797-1828

Franz Peter Schubert was born near Vienna, one of nineteen children. His father and brothers were school teachers. They taught him violin, piano and organ.

Schubert, as a boy, had a beautiful voice. His voice was so clear and bell-like that it won him a scholarship in the Imperial Court Singers choir. During his choir years, Schubert also studied music theory. He played in the

orchestra and eventually was allowed to conduct. In 1813 he obtained a job teaching in his father's school and in 1818 was a piano teacher in the Royal household.

Schubert had many friends who were able to influence monarchs and wealthy patrons who would have been able to offer him a secure position. However, he struggled to maintain his completely free spirit and thereby missed several fine opportunities.

Schubert greatly admired the music of Mozart and Beethoven. He met Beethoven in 1827 and impressed the great Master of the era with his many beautiful works. The next year, the first concert of Schubert's own works was given. It was a success, and he made a fair amount of money. However, his life was one of poverty and struggle. He was in poor health and his constant mental frustrations and worry contributed to his physical condition. He developed typhoid and died at the age of only 31. One year

earlier he had been a torch bearer at Beethoven's funeral. Schubert's major request was that he be buried next to Beethoven.

Schubert developed the Romantic Period's "Art Song" from his own individual inventiveness. The Art Song is a song written for a soloist with piano accompaniment in which the poem, the music and the accompaniment all combine to create a single mood or single effect.

Schubert's art songs fall into three categories: Strophic, Varied-strophic (sometimes called modified strophic) and Through-composed. Strophic means that each stanza is sung to the same melody; varied-strophic means that all the stanzas of the poem have the same melody except when a new or different setting is needed to express a special idea or mood; through-composed means that the music has no structured melodic pattern. Narrative poems best fit this description.

During his short life, Schubert wrote 650 songs, 10 symphonies, 19 piano sonatas, 6 masses, 2 sacred cantatas and many dramatic works. The famous "Unfinished Symphony" is his best known symphonic work. One of his most famous art songs is the *Ave Maria*. He wrote rapidly and with great ease as melody was born within him. Yet he died poor. Schuberts' song writing earned little money for him. In fact, if it had not been for Robert Schumann, many of Schubert's great songs may not have been discovered at all. Schumann found several of Schubert's songs laying on a shelf and took them to Mendelssohn who is credited with making them known to the public.

## RECALL

1. Schubert, as a boy, had a beautiful _____.

2. Schubert greatly admired the music of _____ and _____.

3. He developed the Romantic Period's _____.

4. The Art Song is a song written for a _____ with piano accompaniment in which the poem, the music and the accompaniment all _____ to create a single mood and effect.

5. Schubert wrote over _____ of these songs during his lifetime.

## FELIX BARTHOLDY MENDELSSOHN
## 1809-1847

The parents of Felix Mendelssohn were wealthy when their son was born in Hamburg, Germany. Mendelssohn's mother taught music to her children when they were very young. As a child, Mendelssohn would write music for his entire family, including his brother and two sisters. He invited music lovers to his family's Sunday morning concerts. Mendelssohn even conducted a small orchestra to play some of his original symphonies at these family music gatherings.

By the time he was nine, Mendelssohn had mastered the piano, organ and viola and conducted and composed. By fifteen he had written four operas although none were successful. As an accompanist he met many composers

*Felix Mendelssohn*

including Liszt, Chopin, Schumann and Rossini. He also met the famous German poet, Goethe (Gay-teh). At seventeen he wrote the overture to Shakespeare's, *A Mid-Summer Night's Dream*. Mendelssohn later studied with teachers in Paris and Berlin.

Having discovered the music of Bach, Mendelssohn conducted a performance of Bach's, *St. Matthew Passion* in 1829 which was its first performance since Bach's death eighty years earlier. This started a revival of interest in Bach's music and led to the publishing of new editions of his works. Mendelssohn also revived Schubert's music eleven years after Schubert's death.

Mendelssohn became the conductor of the Gewandhaus Orchestra in Leipzig and set new standards in orchestral performance. In Leipzig, with Schumann, he founded the famed Leipzig Conservatory in 1846.

Mendelssohn's father was a prominent Jewish banker named Abraham Mendelssohn. His grandfather was the famous philosopher Moses Mendelssohn. Mendelssohn's racial heritage created problems for him in Germany. His popularity fell.

Leaving Germany, Mendelssohn went to England where he was welcomed and respected. There, he became a Christian and used his mother's maiden name, Bartholdy (Felix Mendelssohn-Bartholdy). Many of his compositions

are signed using this name.

Mendelssohn returned to Germany from England to face the sad news of his beloved sister's death. The famous composition, *Song Without Words*, was really written by his sister, Fanny. She was reported to be his musical equal. In general, women were not given recognition in the music profession at that time. Constant overwork and the sadness of Fanny's death appear to have hastened Mendelssohn's passing on November 4, 1847.

Unlike other composers of the Romantic Era, Mendelssohn had no money problems. He combined the Romantic Period expression with his own love for the Classical Period. Perhaps his lack of life's traumatic experiences gave his music its class: romantic, light, delicate with symmetrical balance. There is a sort of Polish flavor evident and a sunny, happy disposition which was so characteristic of Mendelssohn's personality.

### RECALL

1. As a child, Mendelssohn would _____ music for his entire family.
2. In Leipzig, with Schumann, he founded the famed _____ _____.
3. Leaving Germany, Mendelssohn went to _____.
4. Many of his compositions are signed using the name _____ _____-_____.
5. The famous composition, "_____ _____ _____", was really written by his sister, Fanny.

## ROBERT SCHUMANN
## 1810-1856

Robert Schumann, born in Zwickau, Germany, was a composer destined to face many tragedies. Like many

*Robert Schumann*

other composers of the Romantic Period, he showed musical ability at the age of seven. By twelve, he could play the piano quite well.

Schumann was known to have been a dreamer. His father had a nervous ailment and his mother was known to suffer from moods. Both of his brothers died at an early age and his sister took her own life by drowning. Schumann's father supported his musical desires although his mother wanted him to become a lawyer. When Schumann's father died, his mother insisted that he go to Leipzig where he could study law. While in Leipzig, he also began to study piano under Friedrich Wieck. Although Schumann went to other universities, including Heidelberg, he still could not completely concentrate on his law course. Later, he went to Italy and still attempted his legal studies.

Finally at twenty, he wrote to his mother and informed her that he was going to study music. He won her consent and returned to Leipzig to study again under Wieck. Wanting complete independence and strength in each finger, Schumann invented a small contraption which would keep one finger still and allow the other fingers to play. This little invention injured his right hand permanently and his hopes for becoming a great pianist vanished. Schumann then turned to the study of composition.

After hearing the new musical genius and concert pianist, Chopin, in 1831, Schumann wrote a very excellent review article about him that introduced Chopin to wider musical circles. The article also created for Schumann many art lovers and friends. The response was so overwhelming that Schumann organized a group which was called the "Davidsbund." This was Schumann's 'League of David'—a group established to uphold the cause of the new romantic style. Schumann's musical taste was shared by all the members of his Davidsbund. 'Philistines' was a term used by Schumann to refer to those musicians or artists who were not up to the League's standards. The League did not respect the old conservative ideas. Schumann signed his critiques three ways—Eusebius, Florestan or Raro. Eusebius was the critic with a great enthusiasm for new works. Florestan pointed out the faults of the performer or artist and Raro was the objective balance between Florestan and Eusebius.

Schumann's musical criticisms came at a time when music critics were receiving little attention. The traditional approach used in writing articles created little interest. Schumann revived interest and inspired both readers and artists.

In 1834 he established an outstanding music newspaper, the "Neue Zeitschrift fur Musik" (The New Journal for Music). Schumann edited this paper for ten years.

In 1836 Schumann became interested in Clara Wieck, the daughter of his teacher. Clara's father was very upset by this relationship as he felt that Schumann was unstable. His daughter was an excellent concert pianist and only seventeen years old and he fiercely opposed their marriage. In 1840 it became necessary for Schumann to obtain consent from the Court of Appeals in order to marry Clara.

Mendelssohn had organized the Leipzig Conservatory in 1843 and Schumann was invited to teach there. However, he was neither a good teacher or conductor and soon moved on to Dresden (1844) and then to Dusseldorf (1850).

Schumann wrote compositions which his wife played and he went along on several tours with Clara. These works were very well received.

In 1853 Schumann wrote an article called "New Paths" in which he spoke of Brahms' genius and bright future. Brahms and the Schumanns became lifelong friends and the Schumanns did much to inspire Brahms. Schumann later found himself overworked and tried to take his life by jumping into the Rhine River. After his rescue, he was placed in an asylum near Bonn, Germany, where he died in 1856.

Clara Schumann and Brahms maintained a close friendship and shared the memories and works of Robert. Clara continued to develop her career and reputation as a virtuoso and pianist, frequently continuing to play her late husband's work.

## RECALL

1. Schumann's _____ supported his musical desires.
2. At twenty, Schumann returned to Leipzig to study under _____ _____.
3. Schumann organized a group called the _____.
4. It became necessary for Schumann to obtain consent from the Court of Appeals in order to marry _____ _____.
5. Schumann wrote compositions which his _____ played.
6. _____ and the Schumanns became life-long friends.

# JOHANNES BRAHMS
## 1833-1897

Johannes Brahms, born in Hamburg, Germany is known as one of the 'big three' composers of German birth. Bach, Beethoven and Brahms have been called the 'Three B's.'

Johannes Brahms

Brahms came from a musical family. His father played the double bass in an orchestra. He did many odd jobs to help his father who was very poor. He was even able to sell some of his music. He studied with Remnyi, the violinist, and also went on a concert tour as his accompanist. During this tour he met Joachim, Liszt and Schumann, all famous composers. He also came into contact with gypsies and observed their music, culture and lifestyle. Surprisingly, after this tour, Brahms concentrated on a study of the classics, such as the works of Beethoven and Bach and appeared only rarely in concert.

Brahms wrote every kind of music with the exception of opera. His mother died when he was thirty two and it is believed that he wrote his famous *Requiem Mass* in her honor. Brahms was over forty before he began his immortal symphonic writings.

His life was very simple. Several times he almost married but never did. He kept a life-long friendship with Robert and Clara Schumann. Their friendship, appreciation and encouragement did much to inspire Brahms. Following Schumann's death, he and Clara remained close friends.

Brahms was a plain, sentimental and quiet man. He is known to have played Bach fugues, transposing them from key to key just for enjoyment.

As the director of the Choral Society of the Prince of Lippe-Detmold, he conducted the seasonal concerts of 1857-1859. In 1863, he conducted the Vienna Singakademie in Austria. Later, he became the conductor of the Gesellschaft der Musik Freunde (1872–1875) which still exists today. He accepted no jobs after 1875.

Brahms refused an honorary Doctorate of Music degree from Cambridge University but accepted an honorary 'Doctorate of Philosophy from the University of Bresian. This degree led to the writing of his famous *Academic*

*Festival Overture* after he learned that he was expected to write something for the University. This overture is based on four known student songs of the universities in Germany—*Wir hatten gebauet ein Stattliches Hags* (We Had Built A Stately House); *Fuchslied* (Fox Song)—the freshman song used for hazing; *Was Kommt dort Von der Hohe (*What comes There From on High); and *Graudeamus igitur* (Wherefore Let Us Rejoice).

Brahms revived the variation form, enriched orchestral instrumentation and furthered the classical trends in music already established by Bach and Beethoven.

Brahms, the great 'philosopher of music' died on April 3, 1897.

His music has been called 'pure' or 'absolute' music (music that is non-programmatic or non-narrative, descriptive or imitative). It can be called music for the sake of music.

Brahms works include many Lieder (German songs), symphonies, short works for orchestra, the Haydn Variation, overtures, concertos, chamber music works, piano compositions, sonatas, a scherzo, a piano quintet, orchestral serenades, the famed *German Requiem* (cantata style), intermezzi, rhapsodies, caprices, ballads and last but not least, waltzes, the most outstanding of which are *The Liebeslieder Waltzer* ("Love Song Waltzes").

## RECALL

1. _____, _____, and _____ have been called the 'Three B's.'
2. Brahms came from a _____ family.
3. Brahms wrote every kind of music with the exception of _____.
4. He kept a life-long friendship with _____ and _____ _____.
5. Brahms revived the _____ form and enriched _____ instrumentation.
6. Name two of Brahms' works: _____ and _____.

# FREDERICK CHOPIN
## 1810-1849

Chopin was acclaimed a child prodigy. His moving melodies and unusual rhythms combined with new harmonies to make his compositions imaginative and expressive.

Chopin's French school teacher father, living in Poland, married a cultured, well educated Polish woman. Frederick Francois Chopin was born to them in Zelazowa, Poland, on March 1, 1910.

Chopin's first music teacher was so impressed by his unusual talent that Chopin was allowed to perform a concerto in public when he was only nine years old. He entered the Warsaw Conservatoire at sixteen and studied with Joseph Elsner. He also had his first musical composition published at sixteen.

Chopin gave concerts in Vienna, Warsaw, Munich and Stuttgart, arriving in Paris in 1831 at the age of twenty. Paris was then known as the great 'Capitol of Art'. Most known great musicians lived there. Chopin met and knew many of them well, including Berlioz, Mendelssohn, Liszt, Bellini, Auber, Meyerbeer, Rossini and Cherubini. Also, in 1831, Robert Schumann wrote a review article about Chopin entiltled, "Hats Off, Gentlemen, A Genius!"

Chopin fell in love with Mme. Aurore Dudevant, a writer and novelist known as 'George Sand.' He became very dependent on this strong, dominant woman who served as his inspiration. (It has, however, been speculated that this seven year affair was not the best thing for his tender personality.) Chopin suffered ill health after contracting consumption at the age of 30 while in Majorca with Sand. After Sand and Chopin separated in 1847, Chopin's health worsened; however he still traveled to England and Scotland for concerts. He returned to Paris in 1849 where he died.

Chopin was very concerned about his country, Poland. Some of Poland had been occupied by Russia, Austria and Prussia around 1795. The anguish and sorrow he felt in his heart was reflected in much of his music.

Chopin has been called 'The Poet of the Piano.' He made the piano a solo instrument. Until Chopin, the piano had served primarily as an instrument in the orchestra. His melodies for the piano are singable and song-like and allow for elaboration.

Many of his melodies also reflect on inspiration of the dance. Chopin did not make use of polyphony or counterpoint in his compositional techniques or harmonic relationships. He did use "rubato" —a flexible use of tempo (speed) by altering the values of written notes. In Chopin's music it must be carefully executed.

Chopin also made use of the pedal on the piano called the 'damper' pedal. This is the first pedal on the right. The damper pedal controls the dampers inside the piano. Dampers are felt material glued to wood strips which strike each piano string. When you strike the string by playing the note, the damper is lifted and the string sounds. When you release the key, the damper covers it, stopping the sounds. Chopin sustained his melody or let it reverberate through the air by frequent use of the damper pedal. This effect is usually recognized as Chopin's.

Chopin himself was a brilliant concert pianist with unbelievable technique. But in preparation for his concerts, which featured mostly his own compositions, Chopin would practice the works of Johann Sebastian Bach.

Chopin was comfortable writing for the piano and most of his works are for this instrument. They include piano sonatas, concertos, mazurkas, waltzes, nocturnes, preludes, piano studies, scherzos, etudes, and polonaises.

*Frédéric Chopin*

## RECALL

1. Chopin was acclaimed a child _____.

2. He had his first musical composition _____ at 16.

3. Chopin has been called the Poet of the Piano. He made the piano a _____.

4. In Chopin's music, what must be carefully executed? _____

5. Chopin was a brilliant _____ _____.

# FRANZ LISZT
## 1811-1886

Franz Liszt, destined to become an outstanding pianist-composer, continued the contribution of Chopin to the piano and did much to further piano playing technique. Liszt was born in Raiding, Hungary, in 1811. His first musical instruction was from his father, an amateur pianist and manager of the wealthy and well-known Esterhazy family estates.

When Liszt was nine years old his piano playing was so impressive that several noblemen agreed to give his father financial support for his musical education, equal to $1,000 a year. Liszt was sent to Vienna to study with famous teachers among whom was Karl Czerny (1791-1857).

At the age of eleven, Liszt was taken to meet the great Ludwig van Beethoven. Liszt worshipped Beethoven and learned to play many of his works. The purpose of the visit, in addition to just having young Liszt meet the great master, was to ask Beethoven to attend a concert to be given by Liszt. Beethoven was fifty two years old, deaf and extremely concerned about his health. When Beethoven was asked to attend the young man's concert, he refused, and Liszt was shaken. However, the night of the concert, the aging master came and the young Liszt quickly recognized him in the audience. Franz Liszt played as never before. At the end of the concert Beethoven went to the stage while the audience was still standing and applauding. There, in front of the audience, he kissed the young pianist on the forehead. Thus, the great master, Beethoven, had acclaimed and approved of the talented pianist for the Vienna public.

In 1826, at the time of his father's death, his financial support ceased. Liszt now had to support his mother as well as himself. They moved to Paris and Liszt had no trouble being welcomed into the highest noble groups. Most of the greatest musicians and artists were his friends. Among them were Chopin, Nicolo Paganini (1782-1840),

the famous violinist, and Hector Berlioz (1803-1869), the composer.

At twenty-eight, Liszt went on a tour of Europe. This tour was very successful and contributed toward his financial well being. He also earned the reputation of the greatest pianist of the times. Liszt's new financial circumstances allowed him to help many a struggling or financially needy artist or promising master musician without accepting a fee. He even contributed money for a monument to Beethoven, his idol, in Bonn, Germany.

In 1849 Liszt became the Director of Music for the Court at Weimar, Germany, where he promoted the works of other composers and was recognized as a great conductor. At that time, Weimar was the center for innovative artists and Liszt conducted operatic works by composers whose musical ideas were not readily accepted. Among them were Wagner (Liszt's daughter was married to Wagner), Anton Rubenstein (1830-1894), Berlioz and Peter Cornelius (1824-1874). Because of Liszt, *Tannhauser*, *Lohengrin*, and other Wagnerian operas received their first performances. When the opera, *The Barber of Baghdad* (1858) by Cornelius, was not accepted by the public at Weimar, Liszt left for Rome.

While in Weimar, Liszt's career as a pianist ended and he started to write large compositional forms. Liszt is responsible for some important instrumental advances: the connecting of movements of music together by using some material which is common to all the movements; the use of extra-musical ideas as an inspiration or an idea for a composition; and although the other composers from the classical and romantic periods helped develop trends in the direction of the symphonic poem or tone poem, Liszt was the developer of this rather free form.

The *symphonic tone poem* is a work for orchestra, of symphonic size, but with only one movement. In this type of work, the orchestra really follows a story and is descriptive in its musical themes. It has musical episodes that are connected in a long single movement. This is program music and usually short informative statements about the works are included on the printed program. The text or subject may range from mythical or historical subjects to a make-believe subject. Liszt wrote thirteen tone poems.

The *rhapsody* is also a creation of Liszt's. This is another free form type composition where several themes, which are generally based on folk music, are put together in a manner that has no set pattern or tempo. The rhapsody reminds one of a mixture (a collage) of themes in different colors, lengths, rhythms and patterns.

While in Rome, Liszt almost became a priest. He did earn the title of "Abbe" or "Father." That title was bestowed upon him by the Pope. He then spent the rest of his life in Rome. Occasionally he returned to Weimar to conduct the Beethoven Festival (1870), to Budapest, Hungary, where he was honorary president of the new National Academy of Music in Hungary, and Bayreuth, Germany, where Wagner had built his opera house. Liszt died there in 1886 after becoming ill while visiting his daughter, Cosima, who was married to Wagner during a Bayreuth Opera Festival.

Liszt wrote over seven hundred works. Among them were concertos, oratorios, symphonic tone poems, rhapsodies, several volumes of piano works, cantatas, masses and orchestral works. Some of his most famous and popular works are his hungarian rhapsodies and the *Mephisto Waltz* and *Les Preludes*.

1. Franz Liszt was destined to become an outstanding _____-_____.

2. Liszt was sent to Vienna to study with famous teachers among whom was _____ _____.

3. At eleven, Liszt was taken to meet the great _____ _____.

4. In 1849, Liszt became the _____ _____ _____ for the Count of Weimar.

5. While in Weimar, Liszt's career as a pianist ended and he started to write _____ _____ _____.

6. The symphonic tone poem is a work for an orchestra of symphonic size but with only _____ _____.

7. The _____ is also a creation of Liszt's.

8. Name two of Liszt's most famous works: _____ and _____.

## GIUSEPPE VERDI
## 1813-1901

Giuseppe Verdi, born in Italy, was almost twenty-six years old before he wrote his first opera. Verdi had prepared himself to be a composer by studying orchestration, composition and conducting. He studied at the most famous opera house in the world, 'La Scala' in Milan, northern Italy.

For thirty-eight years, Verdi continuously developed the opera. His early operas, though excellent, do not reflect the style and remarkable use of voice and action he accomplished around 1851 with his outstanding opera, *Rigoletto*. It is frequently performed in opera houses around the world today.

Giuseppe Verdi

During his early life, the tragedy of the loss of his baby daughter, his son and wife within a three year span (1838-1840) caused Verdi much grief. Between 1840 and 1851 he wrote one unsuccesful and two successful operas. Then, in 1853, Verdi wrote *Il Trovatore* (The Troubadour), a tradegy written in a romantic style. This immensely popular work today requires a large scale (and expensive) production.

Verdi's opera, *La Traviata* (The Outcast), was not well received when first presented, although it has since become very popular and a favorite of opera fans today. Following *La Traviata*, Verdi created *Simon Boccanegra, Un Ballo in Maschera, La Forza del Destino* and *Don Carlos*.

The Verdi opera which is the most popular today is *Aida*. Verdi wrote *Aida* upon an invitation from the Viceroy (king) of Egypt to write an Egyptian opera for the opening of the Suez Canal. Verdi agreed and it is reported that he completed it in only a few weeks. *Aida* is a Grand Opera although it was composed to entertain the Egyptian audience. It is exciting and spectacular and the famed triumphal scene is colorful with a spectacular display of pomp and ceremony. The music and the acting are completely in harmony with the mood.

When Verdi wrote "Aida" he was 56 years old and had already written 23 operas. Two of his most outstanding and difficult operas were composed when he was much older — *Otello* and *Falstaff*. He used Shakespearean plays as a basis for these librettos (the stories).

Verdi's operas require the singers to express the true emotions of their characters through expressive melodies and masterful musical styling. The orchestra plays an accompaniment to the singers and supports them but is cleverly never in competition with them. Verdi's florid passages and decorative musical ideas are a work of musical art.

In addition to his work with opera, Verdi should be remembered for his *Requiem Mass*. It is one of the greatest requiem masses written. Giuseppi Verdi died in 1901.

## GIACOMO PUCCINI
## 1858-1924

Giacomo Puccini was born in 1858 in Lucca, Italy. He studied with the famous opera composer, Amitcare Ponchielli (1834-1886) (*La Giaconda*), at the Conservatory in Milan, Italy. Puccini was a talented writer of operas. He understood the theatre and what was needed to make daily situations come alive on the stage.

Puccini not only mastered the understanding of human emotions but also showed great ability to write for orchestra. His tone color and perfect choice of instruments high-light the particular mood called for in his operas. His melodies are beautiful and lyrical. The stories of his operas range from very serious plots to comedies.

Some of Puccini's operas most often requested and performed are *Tosca, Madame Butterfly* and *La Boheme*. These three operas spread his fame throughout the world. His shorter operas, *Il Tabarro, Sour Angelica,* and *Gianni Schicchi,* were performed in New York as early as 1918. Of the three operas, *Gianni Schicchi* is a comedy opera.

Puccini was injured in an automobile accident in 1903 and it was during his convalescence that he wrote *Madame Butterfly*.

While visiting America in 1909, Puccini was commissioned by the Metropolitan Opera Company to compose an opera. He wrote *The Girl from the Golden West*. (*La Fanciulla del West*) based on our Western life style including a scene where a cowboy rides a horse on stage.

Puccini was considered a romantic-realist. He understood the voice and how to write for it. Like Wagner, he often used short musical motifs to identify certain characters throughout the operas.

Puccini died in Brussels, Belgium in 1924 without completing his last opera, *Turandot*.

## GEORGES BIZET
## 1838-1875

Georges Bizet, a noted French composer, was the gifted son of a professional musician. He studied at the Paris Conservatoire with Marmontel and Gounod.

Bizet's most outstanding work is his opera, *Carmen*, the story of a gypsy girl. His well-structured plan of unfolding the opera plot with such color, vibrancy and action, gives the audience the feeling it is experiencing each character's dilemma.

Bizet wrote many operas and works for orchestra in his short life.

## ENGLEBERT HUMPERDINCK
## 1854-1921

Englebert Humperdinck was born in Germany and studied at the Cologne Conservatory and in Munich. He was greatly impressed by Richard Wagner, the great German composer. Humperdinck assisted Wagner in the production of *Parsifal*.

Humperdinck's best known work is his popular children's opera, *Hansel and Gretel*. The opera's libretto is a fairy story which includes two children, a wicked witch in the forest, a castle and all of the imaginary magic of a fairy tale. The prayer from this opera, called the *Children's Prayer*, is extremely beautiful and touching.

Humperdinck's other works included *The Royal Children*, and music for Shakespeare's plays, *The Winter's Tale* and *The Tempest*.

1. Giuseppe Verdi studied at the most famous opera house in the world, "_____" in Milan.
2. Name two of Verdi's most famous operas:
   _____
   _____
3. _____ was another talented Italian composer of operas.

4. Puccini wrote "_____ _____" during his convalescence.
5. Bizet's most famous opera is "_____", the story of a gypsy girl. He was a famous _____ composer of the Romantic Period.
6. "_____ and _____", a popular children's opera, was written by _____ _____.

## RICHARD WAGNER
## 1813-1883

About the same time as the "Blues" emerged in America, Richard Wagner was born in Leipzig, Germany. At the age of sixteen, he began to show a serious interest in music. By the time he was twenty, he had obtained a job as a music conductor in a theater. More than anything, he wanted to compose his own operas.

Opera is an art form in which most of the arts participate. It is a drama set to music to be performed with scenery, costuming, acting, dancing, solo singer, ensembles and choirs, all accompanied by an orchestra or soloists under the leadership of a conductor. Opera productions usually require a producer, a director, a technical director, and orchestra conductor, a choreographer, a choral director, a publicity director, a costume designer, a make-up artist, a stage crew, a stage director and a set designer.

Wagner developed new techniques for opera. Usually an opera composer followed a libretto (story). Seldom were these texts written by the composer. But Wagner was not content to use the words of others. He wrote his own words and designed his own sets and scenery. He conducted the orchestra, sketched the costumes and organized the performers. He even built an opera house in which his operas could best be performed.

Many musicians claim that Wagner's music marks the beginning of modern music. He weaves in and out of keys, usually in a chromatic manner. One notes his great ability to write soaring and thrilling melodies. His creation of lietmotiv (a short descriptive musical idea) for each character, which was played each time the character appeared, is now often used, even in movies and television. Wagner was fond of fantasy and many of his operas give one the idea of a make-believe world.

Wagner died in 1883 in Venice. He made an impression on the music world which will last forever. Some of his famous operas are, the *Flying Dutchman, Tannhauser, Lohengrin, Die Walkure, Das Rheingold, Tristan and Isolde, Siegfried, Die Meistersinger* and *Parsifal.*

*Richard Wagner*

1. Wagner wanted to compose his own _____.
2. Opera is an art form in which most of the _____ participate.
3. Wagner developed new _____ for opera.
4. He was not content to use the _____ of others.
5. His creation of a _____ for each character is now often used in movies and television.

# THE IMPRESSIONISTIC PERIOD
# 1870-1900

In 1870, France was defeated by Germany in the Franco-Prussian War. There arose a rejection of German culture by the French and a renewed interest in French culture and its promotion. Germany, which had been the center of musical culture, no longer enjoyed this title. France now emerged as the cultural center of Europe and an artistic, intellectual force in Paris became interested in getting away from the strong, passionate, heroic themes of the Romantic Era. Nature, the sea, sunsets, gardens and people at work in the outdoors impressed these painters, poets and musicians. A sensuous expression of nature and its products became the dominant subject of this era.

In an art show in Paris in 1874, Claude Monet exhibited one of his paintings called 'Sunrise' (his impression of the sun rising over the Thames River). The critics of this new school of painting attending the exhibition coined the name "Impressionistic," using it in an uncomplimentary manner. The term caught on and Impressionistic became the official title used to describe the poets, painters and musicians of that era. Its most representative musicians and composers were Claude Debussy and Maurice Ravel. Their works are today among the most expensive in private and museum collections.

Some musical characteristics of this Period are:
1. Muted strings and brass, creating a shimmering effect.
2. Obscure melodies, whole tone scales and irregular phrases.
3. Unresolved dissonance with parallel movements of chords with cadences often concealed.

---

## CLAUDE ACHILLE DEBUSSY
## 1862-1918

Claude Achille Debussy was born in St. Germain-en-Laye near Paris, France. Debussy was a composer who was not willing to accept musical rules and styles handed down to him. He studied piano with Marmontel, harmony with Lavignac and composition with Guiraud. The American composer Edward MacDowell, fifteen years old at the time, was his fellow student.

Debussy was influenced by the master French composer, Massenet. Because he was so interested in experimentation during his college studies at the Paris Conservatoire, he often drifted from the traditional harmonic progressions into dissonant, dreamy types of chords. He eventually created a new sound with tonal progressions which were a definite breakaway from his predecessors.

At the age of twenty two, Debussy wrote a cantata, *L'Enfant Prodigue* (The Prodigal Son) which won the Prix

*Debussy*

de Rome Scholarship. This allowed him to travel to Rome, Italy, for study. He returned to Paris before finishing his studies.

Debussy was musically influenced by several sources:
1. The Russian style of Rimsky-Korsakov with its musical texture timbre and color. (He saw Rimsky-Korsakov conduct a number of concerts in Paris in 1889.)
2. Oriental music—Pentatonic, whole tone and modal scales.
3. Spanish dance rhythms, the habanera and the tango, which his *La Soiree dans Grenade* and *La Serenade Interrompue* reflect.
4. The Symbolist poets such as Baudelaire, Verlane and Mallarme. He used Mallarme's text for his symphonic poem *Prelude a l'apres Midi d'un Faune* (Prelude to the Afternoon of a Faun).
5. The music of the American Black man reflected in Debussy's piano pieces, *The Little Negro* and *Golliwog's Cake Walk,* with syncopated dance rhythms.

*The Afternoon of a Faun* was first performed in 1906 at the Paris Conservatoire and in America in 1907 by the Chicago Symphony Orchestra under Frederick Stock. The opera *Pelleas and Melisande* was performed in New York during the 1907 season at the Oscar Hammerstein Manhatten Opera House with Mary Gardner, the famed American opera star in the role of Melisande. The New York Symphony orchestra played his two nocturnes, *Nuages* and *Fetes,* at Carnegie Hall in 1905 with Walter Damrosch conducting.

Debussy's music is melodic, haunting, dreamy and mystical. He died in 1918 and is remembered as a master composer of the Impressionistic Era.

### RECALL

1. Debussy was a composer who was not willing to accept musical _____ and _____ handed down to him.
2. The American composer _____ _____ was Debussy's fellow student.
3. Debussy eventually created a new sound with _____ _____ which were a definite breakaway from his predecessors.
4. Debussy was musically influenced by several sources. Name three: _____, _____ and _____.
5. "_____ _____ _____ _____ _____" was first performed in 1906 at the Paris Conservatoire and in America in 1907.

# MAURICE JOSEPH RAVEL
## 1875-1937

Another representative impressionistic composer was Maurice Ravel who was born in Ciboure, France, in 1875. Ravel studied at the Paris Conservatoire where his venturesome style of writing resulted in his loss of the Prix de Rome several times. This caused the dismissal of the director of the Conservatoire.

Debussy and Ravel were contemporaries. Ravel was influenced by the Russian musical style—its texture, timbre and color, and composers Emmanuel Chabrier (1841-1894) and Erik Satie (1866-1925).

Ravel employed most of the musical characteristics used by Debussy and defined as impressionistic. However, he made use of a more classic impressionistic style. That is to say, Ravel's melodies were more clearly outlined and he used several classic dance rhythms including the pavane, habanera, bolero and waltz.

Ravel's music seems less dreamy, soft and vague than Debussy's music. He emphasized rhythm in his music while Debussy emphasized tone color.

## RECALL

1. Another representative impressionistic composer was _____ _____ who was born in Ciboure, France.

2. Ravel was influenced by the _____ musical style.

3. Ravel made use of a more _____ impressionistic style.

4. Ravel used several dance rhythms including the pavanne, habanera, _____ and _____.

5. _____ and _____ are remembered as famous French Impressionistic composers.

# SERGEI RACHMANINOFF
## 1873-1943

Sergei Rachmaninoff, the Russian pianist and composer, was gifted with the ability to create hauntingly lyrical melodies which lingered with the listener.

Rachmaninoff's music could best be associated with that of Chopin and Liszt. His music uses embellishments and technical devices and he displayed a virtuosity of exceptional quality. His understanding of the keyboard made him a great composer for the piano.

Rachmaninoff wrote 24 preludes, one in each major and minor key, as did J.S. Bach and Chopin. His *Prelude in C-Sharp minor for Piano* is his most popular piano solo

His four piano concertos are popular with audiences all over the world.

Although Rachmaninoff is most famous for his piano works, he was not limited by them. His music also includes songs and choral and orchestral works.

## RECALL

1. Sergei Rachmaninoff was a Russian _____ and composer.

2. His music could best be associated with that of Chopin and _____.

3. His understanding of the _____ made him a great composer for the piano.

# AMERICA
# 1825-1900

# AMERICA 1825-1900

## Minstrel Shows

Minstrel Shows are recorded as being held in England as early as the 15th century. The English darkened their faces and poked fun at the Africans. In America, however, Minstrel shows didn't begin until about 1820. In this show, white actors (males only) imitated the life style, culture and habits of the Black people (both the slaves and the free). These imitations were done on stage through dancing, singing songs, telling jokes, staging skits and doing acrobatic acts. The accompaniment was provided by instruments such as the Banjo, Fiddle (Violin), Tambourine, Bones and other instruments used by the slaves.

The music used for the minstrel shows was taken from the songs of the slaves. White performers went to the plantations to watch and listen to the daily work routines in the cottonfields. They also went down to the river docks and to the tobacco fields, factories, and out on steamboats. Every small detail of the slaves' movements and music was imitated. Slaves were also taken by wagon from the plantation to various places to entertain the whites.

The Banjo was a favorite instrument of the minstrel show. The first banjo was created by a Black man, Joel Walker Sweeney (1813-1860). Sweeney had a dazzling technique and paved the way for the coming of Ragtime music which followed the Minstel Show era. Joel Walker Sweeney could play his Banjo in any position— behind his back, between his legs and over his head. He favored highly syncopated rhythms.

Sweeney's first Banjo was a wooden box cut in half. One side was covered with skin and five strings were strung over it.

The founder of the minstrel show is said to have been Thomas Dartmouth, "Daddy Rice" (1808-1860), who was later to make famous the role of "Jim Crow."Seeing a black slave at a stable singing and dancing just before going on stage one night, Rice borrowed the slave's clothes, covered his face with burnt cork and imitated the slave's dancing and singing. He was an instant success.

During the 1820's and 1830's many white performers in blackface entertained audiences at circuses, variety halls and fairs. Ensemble groups began to appear in the early 1840's which included banjo players, fiddlers, dancers and singers in varying combinations. From this evolved the larger Minstrel Show which included complete minstrel bands.

The first large group Minstrel Show was given by the Virginia Minstrels on March 7, 1843, in Boston. It was a big success. Several minstrel companies then appeared including the Missouri Minstrels, the Alabama Minstrels and the Kentucky Minstrels. By the year 1846, Bryant's Minstrels, the Christy Minstrels and many other companies had formed. Just about every state had a minstrel company.

The typical minstrel company performers darkened their faces, wore white gloves and painted their lips white. They portrayed two main types of Blacks: The Southern Black called "Jim Crow" (darky), who was poorly dressed or ragged, used heavy dialect and was poor but always happy and jolly in nature. The Northern Black (or city black), then called "Zip Coon" (the dandy), who was dressed well in the latest fashion, was egotistical and always bragging about his female conquests, and who imitated the white man's life style and dress.

The stage position for the minstrel show was a semi-circle. In addition to "Jim Crow" and "Zip Coon" there were other main characters—the Interlocutor or Straightman and the Endmen, Mr. Tambo and Mr. Bones. The remaining cast included dancers and acrobats depending on the size of the company.

The Interlocutor or Straightman was the Master of Ceremonies. He was elegantly dressed and usually in white face. His function was to keep the show moving and to take the jokes, punch lines, statements and comments of the Endmen, Mr. Bones and Mr. Tambo. Mr. Bones played the 'Bones' and Mr. Tambo played the Tambourine. Their remarkes delighted audiences in those days and enhanced the role of the Interlocutor who pretended to constantly try to understand the comments of the Endmen.

Part 1 of the Minstrel Show began with the cast entering playing their instruments, making noise and talking. Then came the Interlocutor's famous words, "Gentlemen, be seated." Constant joking between Mr. Bones and Mr. Tambo and the Interlocutor was carefully inserted between the solos, comedy songs and sentimental type ballads performed by the other members of the cast.

Part II, called the *Oilo*, included many short skits and comedy monologues. In this part of the Minstrel Show, "Zip Coon" and "Jim Crow" were featured. The Olio was often the longest part and it was the forerunner of the later popular Vaudeville Show. Sometimes the Olio was performed in front of the curtain.

In part III, the *Afterpiece*, a parody of a known play was frequently included. *Uncle Tom's Cabin* was one of the most used plays for this purpose. Burlesque was also a major part of the Afterpiece in the Minstrel Show.

Part IV, the final scene, was the *Grand Walk*. The Grand Walk featured all the members of the cast. Each member walked around the stage dancing either the "Juba" or the "Buck and Wing." These dances were performed with great energy, drive and physical exertion.

The Juba Dance called for intricate foot work and it usually also involved the audience. After the Juba Verse by the dancer, the audience would clap its hands, stamp its feet and sing the refrain while struggling to keep up with the driving rhythmic beat of the dancer.

The Buck and Wing dancers were usually costumed in rags and maintained a sort of syncopated jerky boucing of the leg below the knee. The performers often became so involved, they nearly passed out from exhaustion while performing.

Finally, all the performers would play their music and dance around the stage in a circle doing the *Cake Walk*.

The Cake Walk was a high-stepping, elegant dance created by the slaves, which is believed to have originally poked fun at the overly dressed white Southern gentlemen and his courtly gestures. The slaves would usually sing and dance after a hard days work in front of the big house on the plantation. The couple with the grandest strut was awarded a cake by the slave owner, The Massa. The dance therefore came to be known as the Cake Walk. The Cake Walk was also known as the *Ethiopian Cake Walk.*

The solo dance was a very important part of the minstrel show. Many of these solo dances were done to virtually any popular music of the time. The only requirement was that the performer use the exact slave gestures and inflections. *Clog* and *Jig* dancing are two examples of this. Clog dancers usually wore clog shoes and mastered the art of clicking their heels as they danced. The sound was so loud that is said to have scared off dogs when slaves were obtaining food from the fields without permission.

Any comical skit about Black people was called a *Negro Extravaganza.* Longer and larger plays about Blacks were called *Ethiopian Operas.* This was the forerunner of Ballad Operas (English) and of our modern musical comedies.

Blacks were not allowed to perform in minstrel shows although Black entertainers in the North who were not slaves, often entertained white audiences using songs which they call minstrel songs.

Picayune Butle, an early black (non-slave) minstrel singer, is the man who composed an early minstrel song, *Old Zip Coon.* A white circus performer, George Nichols, performed Butle's "Old Zip Coon" in a circus act as *Turkey In the Straw.* This famous title has become a standard American song often assumed to be of white folk origin and seldom revealed to the public as a Black man's creation.

The entire Minstrel Show was presented in a manner which made fun of the Black man. It demeaned and stereotyped him. The early Minstrel Show painted a false picture of a sad people most of whom were in bondage.

## RECALL

1. Minstrel Shows were held in England as early as the _____ century. In America they began about _____.
2. The music used for the minstrel shows was taken from the _____ of the _____.
3. The _____ was a favorite instrument of the minstrel show. It was created by _____ _____ _____.
4. The first large group minstrel show was given by the Virginia Minstrels in 1843 in _____.
5. The typical minstrel company performers _____ their faces, wore white _____ and painted their _____ white.
6. The Southern Black was called "_____ _____" and was _____ dressed.
7. The Northern Black was called "_____ _____" and was _____ dressed.
8. In addition to "Jim Crow" and "Zip Coon" there were other main characters called the Interlocutor or Straightman and the Endmen, Mr. _____ and Mr. _____.
9. The _____ was the forerunner of the later popular vaudeville show.
10. The _____ _____ was a high stepping, elegant dance created by the slaves.
11. _____ were not allowed to perform in minstrel shows.

The Real Cakewalk

# Minstrel Show Writers

The later Minstrel Shows had difficulty gathering music from the slaves. The slaves had become wiser and were aware of the fact that they were being impersonated in a manner of which they did not approve. They realized that they could not participate in these shows because of their race and that, financially, their music and life styles made money for others.

When those seeking new music and ideas came around, the slaves performed only the routine material already known. The minstrel entertainers then had to use any materials they could find from general folk music sources to music from popular operas of the day, to which they simply adopted the slaves' language and gestures. This led to the need for minstrel composers and created the demand for many new popular song writers.

Three outstanding composers of the Minstrel Show Era were Dan Emmett, Stephen Foster and James A. Bland. Dan Emmett usually wrote for the minstrel company as a whole; Stephen Foster wrote mostly for the soloists; James A. Bland wrote for the entire minstrel show, and he was also a world famous minstrel show performer.

## DAN EMMETT
## 1815-1904

Of the hundreds of songs that Dan Emmett wrote, he is best remembered for his composition, *Dixie*. *Dixie* became the anthem of the Southern Confederacy during the Civil War. Dan Emmett originally used *Dixie* for the Minstrel Show walk arounds. No one really remembers the meaning of the word Dixie, since the word was a term used for many years by the slaves during the minstrel era, and nowhere can the slave meaning of the word be found.

Emmett used the word Dixie to mean "this spirited land or country" (America). Although Dan Emmett, Northerner, had written *Dixie*, for the inauguration of Jefferson Davis as head of the Confederacy in Montgomery, Alabama, it became the Confederate Army song and anthem.

Daniel Emmett

# STEPHEN FOSTER
## 1826-1864

Stephen Foster wrote over two hundred beautiful songs. He was greatly influenced in his composing by the music of slaves and the music of the minstrel shows. His songs may be placed into the following categories: Plantation songs—sentimental in style, such as *Old Folks At Home, Old Black Joe, Massa's In De Cold, Cold Ground* and *My Old Kentucky Home;* Ballads—sentimental and descriptive in style like *Jeanie With The Light Brown Hair;* Ethiopian Songs—nonsense songs like *Oh, Susanna, Ring, Ring De Banjo* and *Camptown Races.*

Foster permitted some minstrel writers to add their names to his music before he recognized its popularity and potential. E.P. Christy bought many of Foster's songs outright, often adding an extra five dollars to Foster's pay for permission to substitute his name as the composer. Foster was so poor, that many times he accepted the extra five dollars. *Old Folks At Home* is an example of a Foster song sold outright. Foster later changed his mind but Christy refused to replace his name with Foster's. Foster was sympathetic to the slaves and tried to present them as humans struggling under adverse conditions.

Although Stephen Foster had little musical training, he became one of the American composers to be placed in the Hall of Fame in 1940. He was America's first popular songwriter.

## RECALL

1. The later minstrel shows had difficulty obtaining _____ from the slaves.

2. Two outstanding composers of the minstrel show era are _____ _____ and _____ _____.

3. Dan Emmett's best remembered composition is "_____".

4. Stephen Foster wrote plantation songs, _____ and _____ _____.

5. Name two songs by Stephen Foster: _____ and _____.

6. Stephen Foster became one of the American composers to be placed in the _____ _____ _____ in 1910.

Stephen Foster

# JAMES A. BLAND
## 1854-1911

James A. Bland was one of the greatest writers of American minstrel music. He was a Black composer, banjo player dancer and singer. Bland was labeled "The World's Greatest Minstrel Man" and his fame was not limited to America, but spread to Paris, London, Germany and Scotland.

Born in Flushing, New York, James A. Bland moved to Washington, D.C., with his parents. His father was the first of his race to hold the position of Appointed Examiner in the United States Patent Office. Bland was considered a prodigy. He served as a page in the House of Representatives as a boy and was educated at Howard University. During his early years, he was unable to perform with any leading minstrel troupe because he was Black, so he performed alone at private parties and dances. Bland had become a well-known song writer before he performed with his first minstrel troupe in 1879, the Haverly's Colored Minstrels.

In 1882 Bland went to England and Scotland. He was honored by the Prince of Wales and King Edward several times. He returned to this country in 1910. His style of music was dying out; he was only able to find work in the office of a friend. Disgusted, destitute and unhappy, he moved to Philadelphia where he died on May 5, 1911.

Bland wrote over seven hundred songs; many of them he sold outright. He too, allowed others to attach their names to his music. Many of his songs were sung all over the country by all people. Most never knew Bland's racial heritage. Among the few of his songs available today are *Oh, Dem Golden Slippers, In the Evening by the Moonlight, In the Morning by the Bright Light* and *Carry Me Back to Old Virginny.*

*Carry Me Back to Old Virginny* was published in 1878 and was adopted as the official State song of Virginia in 1940. Several of Bland's songs have been used as marching songs and campaign songs. *Dandy Black Brigade* is an example of one of his marching type songs. Bland's music evoked both tears and laughter. This is truly a mark of a great minstrel composer. *The Sporting Girl,* a musical show in two acts with 18 songs, was his last work.

## RECALL

1. James A. Bland was one of the greatest writers _____ _____ music.

2. He served as a page in the _____ _____ _____.

3. During his early years, he was unable to perform with any leading minstrel troupe because he was _____.

4. Name two of James Bland's songs you remember: _____ and _____.

5. _____ was adopted as the official State song of Virginia in 1940.

# Minstrel Shows After The Civil War

After the Civil War, Black Minstrel Companies began to form. Among the professional groups was the Georgia Minstrels, organized by George Hicks. He eventually had to sell his show because racial segregation kept him out of many theatres and opera houses. The troupe was only able to continue as Callendar's Consolidated Spectacular Colored Minstrel Show because it was operated under white ownership. The Plantation Minstrel Company, Haverly's Genuine Colored Minstrels and McCabe and the Young Minstrels were other minstrel companies of that time.

Small minstrel companies had a difficult time. Racial segregation was always a threat. Signs were posted in Southern towns letting Blacks know their place or warning them to be out of town at a certain time. Places to stay were very hard to find. Usually the performers had to sleep in the particular hall or house rented for the show. The number of band members was often limited and sometimes there was only one banjo player. Often these troups had to resort to advertising the show by going to the working sites at lunch hour to perform excerpts from the show with the hope of enticing workers to attend the evening show.

Still, the Black Minstrel Shows flourished, and the larger well-financed minstrel companies arranged for their performers to travel on special rented trains. On the day of the minstrel show a grand parade was sent through the streets of the city or small town. The parade was a colorful procession with a precise arrangement—carriages in front with the business personnel, then the carriages with the stars of the show in costumes (tall hats and long-tailed coats); the walking segment of the show came next which included comedians, dancers, instrumentalists and singers. This group was also very colorfully dressed. The instrumentalists usually marched in small groups, two or three at a time, making the parade seem longer, Banners were usually carried by local people, preferably younger boys from the visited town or city.

The band instrumentation now included a brass section (cornets, trombones and tuba); woodwind section (flutes, piccolos, clarinets); and a battery (drums of all kinds).

The parade would stop at the city or public square where a short concert of classical music was played. Then the parade would start again and march to the performing hall or opera house. The cast was then free until performance time.

The evening performance was preceded by the band playing. The barker or announcer would then begin the ticket sale. The music and his persuasive announcing had to attract people to attend the show.

During the Minstrel Show performance, many of the instrumentalists played fiddles, guitars, banjos, percussion instuments and mandolins rather than the marching band instruments they had used before the show.

The Black Minstrel Show music was a natural medium for its performers. Many were untrained musicians but could perform the music by ear as well as trained musicians. It became almost impossible to distinguish the trained from the untrained musicians.

The singing voices in the Black Minstrel Show included the natural folk use of the falsetto range that many Black tenors had mastered. The tenors usually performed the ballad-type songs (lyrical, sentimental melodies) while the basses did special songs which showed off the deep, rich register of the bass voice. The comic songs were sung by comedians.

Women were allowed to perform in these Minstrel Shows and Sisseretta Jones, who was a trained singer, made show tours using the name "Black Patti!" Later they were featured in Minstrel Shows billed as The Black Patti Troubadours.

Black minstrel companies also employed a process of apprenticeship for those who wanted to enter the companies. The band leader was the sole responsible member of the troupe. He had the job of selecting, writing and arranging the music for the band. He also trained and taught the vocal groups and soloists writing new music, if necessary. The music ranged from popular songs and spirituals of the Blacks to operatic arias.

**RECALL**

1. After the Civil War, _____ Minstrel companies began to form.
2. Small minstrel companies had difficult times because _____ _____ was always a threat.
3. On the day of the minstrel show a _____ _____ was sent through the streets.
4. The band instrumentation now included a _____ section, _____ section and _____.
5. During the minstrel show performance, many of the instrumentalists played _____, _____, _____, percussion instruments and mandolins.
6. _____ were allowed to perform in these minstrel shows.
7. The music ranged from _____ songs and _____ of the Blacks to operatic arias.

## LOUIS MOREAU GOTTSCHALK
### 1829-1869

Louis M. Gottschalk began studying music at the age of three. When he was six, he became the substitute organist for a church. This young musical genius gave his first public concert when he was eight.

Born in the festival city of New Orleans to a socially prominent family, Gottschalk was exposed to both American and European musical activities. His father was Jewish and his mother a Creole. At the age of thirteen he was sent to Paris where his socially prominent aunt introduced him to the cream of the musical society. Gottschalk studied with the composer, Berlioz.

Berlioz called him an accomplished musician whose playing "dazzled and astonished" his audiences.

Chopin was so impressed with Gottschalk that he predicted he would become "King of the Pianists".

Gottschalk made several concert tours and at sixteen returned to America and gave a concert at the Niblo Gardens in New York. He so impressed the audience with his playing that he was offered an extravagant salary plus all expenses by Claude T. Barnum, who had successfully promoted Jenny Lind, a famous traveling singer. Gottschalk refused the offer but continued to concertize, giving hundreds of concerts all over the United States.

He composed several of his most popular pieces at the early age of fifteen. Among them were *Bambuula* and *La Bananier.*

Gottschalk made many transcriptions of Creole music for the piano. His music was emotional and sentimental, yet pianistic and profound. His tone has been described as "velvet". His rhythms were well defined and he executed them with extreme accuracy. He was very popular in South America and his works also include Black Cuban folk music. Gottschalk's *Le Banjo, Ojos Creollos* and *Last Hope* were included on most of his concert tours.

He was a friend of William Musou, an American musician and piano teacher. Gottschalk was the first American composer/pianist to receive international fame.

**RECALL**

1. Louis M. Gottschalk began studying music at the age of _____.
2. He was exposed to American and _____ musical activities.
3. Gottschalk studied with the composer _____.
4. Gottschalk made many transcriptions for the piano of _____ music.
5. He was the first American composer/pianist to receive _____ fame.

## DUDLEY BUCK
### 1839-1909

Dudley Buck has been considered a pioneer composer writing American musical works for America's musical needs. He was born in Hartford, Connecticut, and because his father really wanted him to become a businessman, he received no musical training as a child.

Buck was sixteen years old before he was allowed to study music. He began his musical studies in Europe, first in Leipzig, then in Dresden and finally in Paris. He returned to Connecticut in 1862 where he obtained a job at the Hartford Park Church as an organist. After several

positions in various churches, he found himself in Chicago. During the great fire of 1871, he was organist at Chicago's St. James Church. It burned to the ground taking with it many of his original manuscripts.

Buck was a fine composer and wrote excellent music for church choir that became very popular at the time and is still popular today.

Buck also wrote well for the organ. His works include several cantatas, shorter songs, ballads, motets and sacred and secular songs.

One of Buck's symphonic cantatas won a prize of $1,000 at the Cincinnati Festival in 1880. Buck's music pleased the public very much and still reflected his own creative ideas. His special gift for melody is evident in his works.

### RECALL

1. Dudley Buck received _____ musical training as a child.
2. He was _____ years old before he was allowed to study music.
3. During the Chicago Fire of 1871, Buck was _____ at the St. James Church.
4. Buck wrote music for the _____ _____.

## JOHN PHILLIP SOUSA
### 1856-1932

John Phillip Sousa, The March King, was the most important American band music composer.

Having served in the Marines where he was director of bands, he organized a professional concert band in 1892 made up of civilains. This "Sousa Band" under Sousa's personal direction, toured the world and lasted forty years.

Sousa, in addition to conducting, wrote original music for his bands and invented the convenient marchers' tuba called the Sousaphone. You can see them in almost every football halftime show in America today.

Many of his marches are still famous and almost everyone in the world knows his most famous, the *Stars and Stripes Forever*. It is played on occasions of state by bands in every country as a salute to America. It was probably the most performed work in the many celebrations of the 1976 American Bicentennial.

### RECALL

1. John Phillip Sousa is known as the _____ _____.
2. John Phillip invented the _____.
3. His most famous march is _____ _____ _____.

## EDWARD MACDOWELL
### 1861-1908

Edward MacDowell is considered the first American composer who was successful in writing music using the larger classical forms. He was born in New York and from childhood showed signs of musical and artistic talent.

During MacDowell's high school years he decided to become a concert pianist. He was sent to Europe to study at the Paris Conservatoire. Claude Debussy also attended the Conservatoire and he and MacDowell studied with several of the same teachers, among them Marmontel. MacDowell then furthered his studies in Germany. While studying, MacDowell also gave private piano lessons, and one of his students later became his wife.

In 1888 MacDowell returned to America where he

taught for a short time in Boston. He went on to New York to become Chairman of the Music Department at Columbia University where he remained until 1904.

A misunderstanding between the college president and trustees served to disturb MacDowell greatly. It is said that his high ideas for the University and his inability to implement them along with overwork led to his death.

MacDowell was an excellent concert pianist and, in addition to teaching, made several concert tours. After his death, his wife conducted tours in America promoting his works. She also established the MacDowell Colony at Peterboro, New Hampshire, where artists may retreat to create without distraction.

MacDowell's works are numerous. Almost everyone has heard his short piano piece, *To A Wild Rose*. His music is descriptive, lyrical and poetic. He made use of the folk idioms of the Earliest Americans and Blacks.

## RECALL

1. Edward MacDowell is considered the first American composer who was successful in writing music using the large _____ _____.

2. MacDowell went to New York to become the Chairman of the Music Department at _____ University.

3. He made use of the folk idioms of the _____ _____ and _____.

## THE FISK JUBILEE SINGERS

The Fisk Jubilee Singers presented the Spiritual (1871-1878) to the world. This small group of nine singers was conducted by Mr. George L. White. He had been hired by the trustees of Fisk University (est. 1866 in Nashville, Tennessee). In his early concerts Mr. White produced outstanding programs which included cantatas, anthems and other major works. The vocal training and technique of this group was exceptional, especially for a group of lay musicians. The Fisk Singers were the first to present Blacks in a serious musical role other than as minstrels.

Though the harmony of the group was plain (using mostly primary triads and dominant seventh chords), the music was beautiful and touching. The basic scale was pentatonic with the diatonic scale used only occasionally. Dialect was used only when the musical need demanded it.

Upon leaving America on their first tour, The Fisk Jubilee Singers visited England, Scotland and Ireland. They appeared before Queen Victoria who was deeply moved by the young singers. Their second tour took the singers to Holland, Switzerland and Germany. The language difference was no barrier as the quality and worth of this new music charmed the listeners. The singers enjoyed rave reviews everywhere they performed.

Many European and English musicians found it difficult to believe that the so-called "Negro" could create such lovely and musically influential art forms. Thus, musicians readily concluded that the Negro must have plagarized the White hymns of the churches in America. Immediate research was started only to discover that this was not the case and that, in fact, many songs and hymns used in England had been borrowed from African melodies. Among them was a very popular Sunday school hymn, *There Is A Happy Land Far Away*. The Fisk Jubilee Singers brought to the world of music a distinct place for the Black man's music. The singers also brought back the sum of one hundred and fifty thousand dollars to their University.

## RECALL

1. The _____ _____ _____ presented the Spiritual to America.
2. The Fisk Singers were the first to present _____ in a serious musical role.
3. The harmony of the group was _____.
4. It was discovered that many songs and hymns used in England had been borrowed from _____ melodies.

## HARRY T. BURLEIGH
## 1866-1949

Harry Thacker Burleigh was born in Erie, Pennsylvania, on December 2, 1866. His mother was a maid and often had to take her son with her to the home of the Russell's where she worked. Frequently the guests appearing or performing at the Russell's were outstanding professional musical artists. Young Harry Burleigh was able to see and hear them. He later became doorman at the Russell home and continued to meet famous artists.

*H. T. Burleigh*

While attending high school, Burleigh sang with many choirs and groups in his community. He also sang at Erie hotels. This gave him the vocal experience which enabled him to win a scholarship in 1892 to the National Conservatory of Music in New York City.

Burleigh studied with and aided the famed Bohemian composer, Antonin Dvorak, who founded and taught at the National Conservatory. He was also a music copyist for Dvorak in New York.

By this time, Burleigh had become an excellent singer and in 1894 he became the baritone soloist at the St. George Church in New York. The congregation was divided over the hiring of the Black singer; however, the majority of the congregation approved through their presence. In 1900 Temple Emmanuel, in New York City, chose Burleigh as its soloist. Burleigh was able to keep both of his church jobs for ten years.

Burleigh was only two years old when the Fisk Jubilee Singers began their European tour introducing the Black Spiritual to the world. Burleigh's profound understanding of his folk heritage and his genius combined with his study with outstanding musicians and composers, all account for a series of brilliant arrangements of Black Spirituals and other creative works. Burleigh's arrangements treated with respect the original folk melodies which he never altered. He had an understanding of the balance needed between phrasing and text. He made them complement each other. His accompaniments fit each arrangement so adequately that one felt they had always been there. Yet, Burleigh's harmonies reflect a European flavor.

Burleigh arranged over fifty Spirituals, thus establishing a place on the concert for the solo Spiritual, an accepted form of folk music created by the Black slaves. These arrangements could be used by amateur and professional choirs and soloist. Thus the "arranged" Spirituals took on a structured form though keeping their folk elements. He also wrote many solo songs which fall into the 'art song' category, among them, *Little Mother of Mine, A Corn Song, Her Eyes, Just Because, The Grey Wolf, Saracen Songs* and *Young Warrier*.

Burleigh worked as an editor for a publishing company, wrote volumes of ballads and spirituals and edited books which includes songs by Stephen Foster. Burleigh received many awards, among them the Spingarm Award, for his contribution to Black music. He died in 1949 in Stamford, Connecticut, at the age of 83.

## RECALL

1. Harry T. Burleigh won a scholarship in 1891 to the _____ _____ of Music in New York City.
2. He studied with and aided the famed Bohemian composer _____ _____.
3. Burleigh arranged over fifty _____.
4. He taught Dvorak the Black spirituals which are included in the "_____ _____ _____".

# ROBERT NATHANIEL DETT
## 1882-1943

Robert Nathaniel Dett was born in Drummondsville, Quebec in 1882. He studied at O.W. Halstead Conservatory in New York and at Oberlin Conservatory, receiving a Bachelor of Music degree in 1908.

An excellent concert pianist, Dett toured America giving concerts and later became the Director of Music for the Hampton Institute of Virginia where he stayed for eighteen years.

In 1920 Dett took a leave of absence from Hampton and traveled to France to study with Nadia Boulanger of the American Conservatory at Fontainebleu. When he returned to America, he taught part-time at several Black colleges and also maintained a private music studio in Rochester, New York.

Dett never ceased to compose. Among his most popular works are two oratorios: *The Ordering of Moses* (1937) and *The Chariot Jubilee* (1921). *The Ordering of Moses* was performed for the Cincinnati Festival of 1927, the Worchester Mass Festival of 1938, the Oratorio Society in New York in 1939 and at Carnegie Hall in 1941 by the National (then called Negro) Opera Company.

Dett's other works include his five piano suites: *Magnolia* (1912), *Enchantment* (1922), *In the Bottoms* (1926), *The Cinnamon Tree* (1928) and *Tropic Winter* (1938) and range from large choral compositions to unlimited arrangements of Black Spirituals. Two collections of Spirituals arranged by Dett were collected by the outstanding opera composer Clarence Cameron White: *Religious Folksongs of the Negro* (1926) and *The Dett Collection of Negro Spirituals* in four volumes (1936).

Dett received various awards, among them the Harmon Foundation Award for Composition in 1927, an honorary Masters of Music degree from the Eastman School of Music and an honorary Doctorate in Music from both Oberlin Conservatory and Harvard, and the Palm and Ribbon Award from the Royal Belgian Band in Europe.

The Columbia Broadcasting Company commissioned Dett to write a work in 1928. However, it was the Australian composer-pianist Percy Grainger (1882-1961) who played and helped bring Dett's piano music to the attention of the American public.

## RECALL

1. Robert Nathaniel Dett was an excellent concert _____.

2. He traveled to France to study with Nadia _____.

3. _____ _____ played and helped bring Dett's piano music to the attention of the American public.

# WILLIAM L. DAWSON
## 1899-

William L. Dawson was born is Anniston, Alabama. He attended Tuskegee Institute, the Horner Institute of Fine Arts in Missouri and the American Conservatory of Music in Chicago where he received his masters degree.

A composition he wrote won first place in a compostion contest and was selected to be performed on the graduation program. It was both a sad and joyous occasion for him. Because of his race, he was seated in the balcony during the program and at the conclusion of the playing of his composition, he was not allowed to walk across the stage to receive the recognition he deserved. (Composers, when known to be present at a performance, are usually recognized at the completion of their works.)

Dawson became director of the music department at Tuskegee Institute where he founded and developed the famed Tuskegee Choirs. They were constantly in demand all over the world and have performed in the White House, on radio and in noted concert halls. The Tuskegee Choirs performed much of Dawson's music and also recorded

many of his works. It was Leopold Stokowski (1887- ), the noted conductor, who recognized Dawson's genius. Stokowski performed Dawson's *Folk Symphony No. 1,* based on Black Spirituals, which introduced Dawson's music to the symphonic world. This symphony was then broadcast over network radio and was performed frequently by the Philadelphia Orchestra. His *Scherzo for Orchestra,* a trio for violin, cello and piano, and his *Sonata for Violin and Piano* are among his best works. Dawson is widely known for his authentic arrangements of Spirituals.

Dawson is still in great demand as a guest conductor, lecturer, composer and teacher.

## RECALL

1. William L. Dawson attended Tuskegee Institute, the Horner Institute and the _____ _____ of Music in Chicago.
2. Dawson became director of the music department at Tuskegee Institute where he founded and developed the famed _____ Choirs.
3. Leopold Stokowski performed Dawson's "_____ _____ No. 1" with the Philadelphia Orchestra.
4. Dawson is widely known for his authentic arrangements of _____.

# MODERN AMERICA

# The Musical Theatre From 1900

# MODERN AMERICA
## The Musical Theatre
## From 1900

## Vaudeville

Vaudeville was derived from the "Olio" section of the Minstrel Show. After the Civil War, Vaudeville shows consisted of songs, dances, slapstick comedy and skits (much like a talent show).

Vaudeville shows became the main source of entertainment during the "Gay Nineties" (1890's) and began to fade out with the coming of motion pictures. Tradition at the time, dictated that vaudeville was not suitable entertainment for women, and door prizes were offered in an effort to get women to attend.

Tony Pastor was one of the great vaudeville entertainers and playing in the Pastor theatre in New York, became the goal of every vaudeville performer. The shows eventually included many blues singers. The great reputations that grew out of these shows included those of Bessie Smith, Eddie Foy, Lillian Russell and George M. Cohan.

### GEORGE M. COHAN
### 1878-1942

George M. Cohan

One of the most popular song writers of the Gay Nineties was George Michael Cohan, born July 3, 1878, in Providence, Rhode Island. At the age of 9 he joined his parents' vaudeville act billed as The Four Cohans.

George M. Cohan became a composer, author, producer, director and performer. He worked on developing a popular form of American musical theatre now known as musical comedy. Some of Cohan's many Broadway musicals were *Little Johnny Jones, Little Nellie Kelly, Forty-five Minutes From Broadway* and *The Man Who Owns Broadway*. The most popular of his songs are *You're A Grand Old Flag, I'm A Yankee Doodle Dandy, Give My Regards To Broadway,* and *Over There*. His unforgettable *Over There,* written in 1912, became the most popular song of World War I. He was awarded the Congressional Medal of Honor for his patriotic songs. It was presented by President Franklin D. Roosevelt.

Cohen died in 1942. He was also honored by a film biography *Yankee Doodle Dandy* and a statue of him stands in Times Square in New York.

**RECALL**

1. Vaudeville was derived from the _____ section of the minstrel shows.
2. _____ _____ was one of the great vaudeville entertainers.
3. The shows eventually included many _____ singers.
4. George M. Cohan was a composer, author, producer, director and _____.
5. He created a popular form of American _____ _____.
6. "_____ _____" became the most popular song of World War I.
7. He was awarded the Congressional _____ _____ _____ for his patriotic songs.

## Tin-Pan Alley

Harry Von Tilzer (1872-1946), a songwriter who became a publisher, was visited by a newspaper reporter. The reporter, Mr. Rosenfeld, noticed an upright piano in Von Tilzer's office stuffed with strips of paper. This gave the music a tinny sound. In his story, the reporter referred to the entire street of music publishers and writer-arrangers as "Tin-Pan Alley".

The slogan "anything to sell a song" was the theme of the Tin-Pan Alley song plugger business at the turn of the century. This business developed in New York around Sixth Avenue and Broadway. From Tin-Pan Alley came the great music industry of today. Tin-Pan Alley developed production line techniques in music. It combined the efforts of song writers—those who composed the tunes; lyricists—those who authored the words; and arrangers—those who wrote down the music adding harmonies and accompaniments. The Tin-Pan Alley producers even took themes from classical music, added lyrics and popular arrangements to them, and sold them as new songs.

Tin-Pan Alley is also thought to have oversold and over-supplied the public with commercial ragtime music. As the public tired of too much in one style, ragtime began its decline.

The quality of commercially produced music has changed and Tin-Pan Alley has expanded from its location in New York to music capitals around the world. Many of the songs of the past live on. Irving Berlin (1888 -    ) wrote many of his tunes in Tin-Pan Alley offices and George Gershwin (1898-1937) was once a song plugger in Tin-Pan Alley.

## IRVING BERLIN
## 1888-

Irving Berlin received very little musical training and found it difficult to put his own music down on paper. He was born in Temun, Russia, and came to America with his family when he was a year old. He grew up on the Lower East side of New York and worked as a singing waiter, and for Harry Von Tilzer, as a song plugger.

His *Alexander's Ragtime Band* made him an instant success. He wrote musical shows for the Ziegfield Follies. Many popular songs came from his musical and film scores such as *Call Me Madam, Annie Get Your Gun, Sayonara, Easter Parade,* and *White Christmas.*

Among his most popular songs still played and sung today are *A Pretty Girl Is Like A Melody, Blue Skies, God Bless America* (for which he received the Congressional Medal of Honor), *White Christmas* (the 1942 Academy Award winner) and *Sayonara.*

## GEORGE GERSHWIN
## 1898-1937

George Gershwin will always be referred to as an American composer who combined jazz and classical music. Gershwin was born in Brooklyn, New York, in 1898 to Russian immigrant parents. He was a song plugger in Tin-Pan Alley when, in 1919, he had his first hit, *Swanee.* Most of his popular songs were written for the Broadway stage.

In 1924, Paul Whiteman, the famous band leader, asked Gershwin to write a jazz piece for his band's concert tour. Gershwin wrote his *Rhapsody in Blue,* a jazz concerto for piano and orchestra. It took him only ten days to complete it. It was orchestrated by Ferde Grofe, the arranger for the Paul Whiteman Band at the time, and brought Gershwin fame.

Gershwin went to Paris with the idea of studying serious composition. He was so taken by this city and its mood that he began *An American in Paris,* a tone poem for orchestra (and never found time for study). "An American in Paris" was premiered in New York in 1928 by the New York Philharmonic with Walter Damrosch conducting.

Gershwin received the Pulitzer Prize for his Broadway stage score *Of Thee I Sing (Baby),* a satire on government officials.

Gershwin's greatest success came with the folk opera, *Porgy and Bess.* An opera combining jazz and classical music, *Porgy and Bess* is based on Dorothy and DuBose Heyword's (1885-1940) play *Porgy.* George's brother, Ira, (1896-   ) collaborated on the lyrics. *Porgy and Bess* is about Blacks who lived around Charlston, South Carolina, and spoke a dialect called "Gullah." Gershwin wanted to be as original as possible and visited the area. He spent weeks making sure he understood the language (dialect) and the musical idioms of the blacks. This is without a doubt, Gershwin's greatest work. Gershwin finished *Porgy and Bess* in 1935, two years before his death. It was premiered in Boston in September of 1935 and produced at the Alvin Theatre in New York in October. It was not immediately successful because many critics found it hard to classify. Some called it a folk opera, some said it was a grand opera and some reviewed it as a musical comedy. Much later some even said it was the model for establishing a true American school of opera. The opera was revived in 1938 and again in 1942 with great success. From 1952 to 1956 *Porgy and Bess* toured many countries in Europe.

George Gershwin had studied orchestration with Rubin Goldmark and was an excellent pianist. His melodies are romantic in texture and his combination of these melodies with jazz harmonies and rhythms created a true American product.

Thanks to Gershwin our own popular musical jazz idioms were written out in classical forms and presented on the concert stage. Gershwin paved the way for comtemporary composers to use the popular jazz American idioms in their writing.

## RECALL

1. The slogan 'anything to sell a song' was the theme of _____ _____ _____.

2. Tin-Pan Alley developed _____ _____ techniques in music.

3. _____ _____ wrote many of his tunes in Tin-Pan Alley and _____ _____ was once a song plugger.

4. Irving Berlin received very _____ musical training.

5. His "_____ _____ _____" made him an instant success.

6. Name two of his songs still played and sung today: _____ _____

7. George Gershwin will always be referred to as the American composer who combined _____ and _____ music.

8. His first hit was "_____".

9. Paul Whiteman asked Gershwin to write a jazz piece for a concert tour. It was the famous "_____ _____ _____".

10. What is the title of Gershwin's greatest folk opera? _____ _____ _____.

## PAUL WHITEMAN
## 1890-

Paul Whiteman might be classified as a Symphonic Jazz conductor. His orchestra played the music of the day in symphonic style. Whiteman's father was a supervisor of music in the public school system and let Paul begin his musical career by studying the violin at an early age.

In his late twenties, he played for dances and soon became the leader of a dance band. Many famous singers got their start as part of his group, including Bing Crosby. In 1924 at the Aeolin Hall in New York City, Paul Whiteman premiered George Gershwin's *Rhapsody in Blue*.

## FERDE GROFE
## 1892-1972

The American composer and arranger who became most noted for his orchestation of George Gershwin's *Rhapsody in Blue* for the Paul Whiteman's orchestra was Ferde Grofe. Grofe's most famous work, however, is his *Grand Canyon Suite* written in 1931 and a regular part of modern orchestra repertory.

## RECALL

1. Paul Whiteman might be classified as a _____ _____ conductor.

2. What famous singer started with Paul Whiteman?
_____ _____

3. Paul Whiteman premiered George Gershwin's "_____ _____ _____".

4. Who orchestrated *Rhapsody in Blue* for Paul Whiteman?
_____ _____

5. _____ _____ _____ is Ferde Grofe's most famous work.

## MORTON GOULD
## 1913-

Morton Gould, composer, conductor, pianist and arranger, was a child prodigy. He was born in Richmond Hill, New York, and was only four years old when he began composing. A waltz of his was published when he was only six years old.

Gould gave virtuoso piano concerts when he was quite young and graduated from New York University when he was fifteen. He was an adept artist with orchestral instruments.

As a young adult he found it necessary to work in order to survive and he played in Tin Pan Alley. Later, in New York, he became a staff arranger for the Radio City Music Hall and then for the National Broadcasting Company. Gould eventually became a leading conductor and worked in radio as a music director.

He made use of the popular American musical styles and clothed them in serious music forms. Among his works are *Spirituals for Orchestra, Jericho* and *Ballad for Band*. The *Spiritual for Orchestra* was inspired by American Folklore. Actual spirituals are not used but Gould writes the melodies in the style and fervor of the Spiritual. He also makes use of a string choir in the manner in which a vocal choir would be used: antiphonal effects are used between the string choir and the orchestra.

Other works of Gould include *Latin American Symphonette, Dance Variations for Two Pianos and Orchestra,* symphonies, film and television backgrounds and stage scores.

## RECALL

1. Morton Gould began composing when he was _____ years old.

2. Some of his works have been called _____.

3. He became a staff arranger for Radio _____ _____ _____.

4. Name a work by Morton Gould:
_____

# LIGHT OPERETTA —
# BROADWAY MUSICALS

One of the true American musical forms to develop from American musical culture is the Broadway musical show or musical comedy.

Traditionally, these plays are first "tried out" outside of New York, then produced on Broadway (New York) and if successful, taken on tour throughout the states. The trend with the more successful musicals has been to write and produce a movie based on the musical.

These shows grew out of the early minstrel-vaudeville shows. They usually have uncomplicated plots, light music, dancing, glamorous costumes, vivid scenery and a mood of excitement. They are usually written by a team of a lyricist and a composer although an individual sometimes writes both the lyrics and the score.

Some of the shows border on the edge of a light operetta when the music is difficult enough to require singers who have had professional training such as *Naughty Marietta* and *Sweethearts* by Victor Herbert and *Maytime, The Student Prince* and *The Desert Song* by Sigmund Romberg.

Shows classified as Broadway musicals are:
*No, No Nanette* - Vincent Youmans
*Of Thee I Sing* - George Gershwin
*Roberta* - Jerome Kern
*Anything Goes* - Cole Porter

*This Is The Army* - Irving Berlin
*Oklahoma* - Rodgers and Hammerstein
*On The Town* - Leonard Bernstein
*Carousel* - Rodgers and Hammerstein
*Annie Get Your Gun* - Irving Berlin
*Brigadoon* - Lerner and Loewe
*Kiss Me Kate* - Cole Porter
*Lost In The Stars* - Kurt Weill
*South Pacific* - Rodgers and Hammerstein
*The King And I* - Rodgers and Hammerstein
*Top Banana* - Johnny Mercer
*The Pajama Game* - Richard Adler
*Mame* - Jerry Herman
*The Most Happy Fella* - Frank Loesser
*My Fair Lady* - Lerner and Loewe
*The Music Man* - Meredith Willson
*Fiddler On The Roof* - Sheldon Harnick and Fred Bock
*West Side Story* - Leonard Bernstein

*The Sound Of Music* - Rodgers and Hammerstein
*Hello Dolly* - Jerry Herman
*Man Of LaMancha* - Mitch Leigh and Joe Darion

## RECALL

1. One of the true musical American forms to develop from American culture is the Broadway musical shows or _____ _____.

2. These shows grew out of the early _____ _____ shows.

3. Some of these shows border on the edge of _____ _____.

4. What musicals have you seen?
   _____
   _____

## VICTOR HERBERT
## 1859-1924

Of the light operetta composers, Victor Herbert stands out as one of the greatest. An excellent musician, Herbert came to America from Dublin, Ireland, in 1886. He studied in Germany and was a fine cellist. Herbert married an opera star who may have influenced his writing style.

He wrote two serious operas before he ventured into writing light operettas. He wrote over thirty-nine light operettas, among them *Babes in Toyland, Sweethearts, The Fortune Teller* and *Naughty Marietta.*

Herbert conducted the Pittsburgh Symphony Orchestra until 1904 when he recruited his own orchestra. He was one of the founders of ASCAP (The American Society of Authors, Composers and Publishers) and also served as a director and vice-president.

## SIGMUND ROMBERG
## 1887-1951

Another outstanding light operetta composer was Sigmund Romberg, a Hungarian-American. Romberg was born in Nagy Kaniza, Hungary, in 1887 and was educated for a career in engineering while studying music as a hobby.

He came to the United States in 1909 and became a citizen in 1912. Romberg had been a pianist and dance orchestra leader. His operetta *Maytime*, written in 1917, established him as an outstanding operetta composer. He wrote over seventy operettas, including *The Student Prince, Rosalie, The Desert Song, Up In Central Park* and *Blossom Time.* Romberg died in New York on November 9, 1951.

## RECALL

1. Of the light operetta composers,
   _____ _____
   stands out as one of the greatest.

2. "Babes _____ _____"
   was written by Victor Herbert.

3. He was one of the founders of
   _____.

4. Sigmund Romberg's operetta
   "_____" established him as an
   outstanding operetta composer.

5. Name a second operetta written by Romberg:
   _____

## LORENZ HART
### 1895-1943

Lorenz Hart, a lyricist, collaborated with Richard Rodgers as part of the team of Rodgers and Hart for over 20 years. They wrote over twenty-five shows, among them *A Connecticut Yankee* (1927) and *Pal Joey* (1940).

Some of his outstanding lyrics are found in the popular songs in *Where Or When, My Funny Valentine, The Lady Is A Tramp, Manhattan* and *With A Song In My Heart.*

## OSCAR HAMMERSTEIN II
### 1895-1960

Born in New York City, Oscar Hammerstein II also shared a writing partnership with Richard Rodgers. As the lyricist, they were known for their great contribution to the American musical theatre.

Hammerstein developed the script for *Show Boat* (Jerome Kern). He was awarded the Pulitzer Prize and two Academy Awards. Some of his most famous musicals are *Oklahoma* (1943), *Carousel* (1945), *South Pacific* (1949), *The King and I* (1951) and *The Sound of Music* (1959).

## RICHARD RODGERS
### 1902-

One of the most successful and important composers for the American theatre, Richard Rodgers was also the most influential. He established new styles, trends and contents in his shows along with both lyricists, Hart and Hammerstein.

Rodgers was born in New York on June 8, 1902 and attended Columbia, Hamilton and Brandeis Universities, the Juilliard School of Music and the University of Massachusetts.

Rodgers was awarded the Pulitzer Prize for *Oklahoma* and *South Pacific;* he was presented Tony Awards for *South Pacific, The King and I, The Sound of Music,* and *No Strings.*

*Richard Rodgers*

## RECALL

1. Lorenz Hart, a lyricist, collaborated with
_____ _____.

2. Name one of his tunes or shows:
_____

3. Oscar Hammerstein II and Jerome Kern wrote the script for "_____
_____".

4. Name two other musicals he wrote lyrics for:
_____
_____

5. Richard Rodgers established new styles, trends and _____ _____ in his shows.

6. He was awarded the Pulitzer Prize for *Oklahoma* and "_____
_____".

## JEROME KERN
### 1885-1945

Jerome Kern, another of America's musical comedy writers, is best known for his *Show Boat,* written in 1927. This was the first musical show written which could have been based on a true life situation. Some of the most memorable tunes from this show are: *Can't Help Lovin' That Man, Bill, Why Do I Love You, Make-Believe* and *You Are Love* and *Old Man River.*

Another of his famous musical Shows, *Roberta,* includes one of his most famous songs, *Smoke Gets in Your Eyes.* Kern won two Academy Awards for *The Way You Look Tonight* (1936) and *The Last Time I Saw Paris* (1941). His first musical hit, *Very Good, Eddie* which he wrote in 1915, was revived on Broadway in 1976.

Kern was born in New York City and was a charter member and director of ASCAP.

*Jerome Kern*

## COLE PORTER
## 1891-1964

Cole Porter studied in Paris and at Yale and Harvard. Although fairly wealthy, he worked hard to become a successful composer.

He wrote over twenty-nine musical shows. Most of his songs are so beautiful and lyrical that the audience leaves singing or humming the melodies as if they belong to them. Among his many wonderful songs are: *Begin the Beguine,*

*Just One of Those Things, Night and Day, I Get a Kick Out of You* and *You're the Top.*

He received the Tony Award in 1948 for *Kiss Me, Kate,* a musical comedy. Other Porter shows include *Can Can* and *Silk Stockings.* Porter also wrote the scores for the films *High Society* and *True Love* and scored music for Kurt Weill.

## BUDDY DESYLVA
## 1895-1950

Buddy DeSylva's real name was George Gard DeSylva. He produced Broadway shows and was a major producer and one of the first composers for Hollywood films.

He started a musical publishing business with Ray Henderson and Lew Brown, both composers, in 1925. Together they wrote scores and scripts for many Broadway musical shows. Some of their hit songs were: *Button Up*

*Your Overcoat, April Showers, The Best Things in Life Are Free, The Birth of the Blues* and *You're the Cream in my Coffee.*

DeSylva wrote mostly the lyrics and shared the script writing with his partners. He collaborated on lyrics for such tunes as *Somebody Loves Me* with Gershwin and *Look for the Silver Lining* (Kern).

## HAROLD ARLEN
## 1905-

Harold Arlen is the composer of *Somewhere Over The Rainbow* from the movie *The Wizard of Oz,* written with E.K. Harburg.

Arlen and Ira Gershwin together wrote *The Man That Got Away.* Some of Arlen's other songs are *One More for my Baby* and *That Old Black Magic* and *Get Happy* in collaboration with Ted Koehler.

Arlen also wrote musical scores for Broadway shows: *Bloomer Girl, St. Louis Woman, House of Flowers* and *Jamaica.*

Arlen was born in Buffalo, New York, in 1905 and sang in a choir in a synagogue, played piano in night clubs and on lake steamers, organized his own band and played in a pit orchestra before becoming a composer and author.

## HOAGLAND HOWARD (HOAGY)
## CARMICHAEL
## 1899-

Hoagy Carmichael was born in Bloomington, Indiana. Although known as a composer, he began his career in the 1920's and '30's as a singer and pianist. He performed with Louis Armstrong, the Dorsey Brothers and many other

popular groups of the day. He also appeared in several movies.

He is best known for his famous *Star Dust,* which was first published as a piano solo without words in 1929, *Georgia on my Mind* and *Lazy River* in 1931.

## RECALL

1. Jerome Kern was best known for his
"_____ _____".

2. "Kiss Me, Kate" and "Can Can" were written by
_____ _____ .

3. Buddy _____ was one of the first composers for Hollywood films.

4. Harold Arlen is the composer of
"_____ _____
_____ _____".

5. What is Hoagy Carmichael's most famous song?
_____

## JESTER HAIRSTON

Jester Hairston is one of todays most popular composers and choral conductors. Hairston's career in professional music began in the Broadway Show, *Hello Paris,* starring the late Chic Sale, in 1930. He then became assistant conductor of the then-famous Hall Johnson Choir in 1936. Hall Johnson and Jester Hairston did the choral arrangements for the Dimitri Tiomkin music in the movie, *Lost Horizons.*

The State Department has sent Hairston as a goodwill ambassador, three times to Africa and twice to Europe in the past ten years. Jester Hairston's choral arrangements of Afro-American folk songs and his own compositions based on folk themes, have been popular among music educators for more than two decades. He is in constant demand as a choral clinician and lecturer.

## RECALL

1. Jester Hairston is best known to musicians
as a _____ and choral
_____

2. He is a specialist with choral arrangements
of _____ folk songs.

# EUROPE

# The Nationalistic Period & Expressionist School in Music 1900-

# EUROPE

## The Nationalistic Period in Music
## 1900-

## Russia

Both the French and American revolutions served as inspiration for a group of composers called *nationalistic*. Their music reveals their intense loyalty, interest and faith in their country.

The spirit of nationalism, or patriotism, has been expressed during all musical periods but reached its peak during the early 19th century.

In Russia, five men sought to develop a Russian school of music. These were Cui, Balakirev, Borodin, Moussorgsky and Rimsky-Korsakoff. They each were aware of the abundance of Russian Folk music and sought to draw their inspirations from this source.

**Cesar Cui** (1835-1918) was an army engineer who eventually became Lieutenant-General. His musical works are not well known and are seldom performed.

**Mily Balakirev** (1837-1910) did intensive research and made available valuable Russian folk songs and dances. As the leader of the group, he constantly encouraged the other four to write. His music is not widely known or performed.

**Alexander Borodin** (1833-1887) was a chemistry professor who actively taught chemistry. He was also a gifted composer who played the piano and the cello. He is noted for his outstanding opera, *Prince Igor*. Borodin worked on this opera for a number of years but it was completed by his friends Rimsky-Korsakoff and Glasounov. It is considered a masterpiece and its characters and music strongly reflect the spirit of the Russian people. The famed *Polovetsian Dances* is found in the second act.

Several of Borodin's works are still heard today.

**Modeste Moussorgsky** (1839-1881) resigned from the army, where he was a junior officer of the guard, to write music. Inspired by Balakirev whom he met in the service, Mourssorgsky became one of the most talented and creative composers among the five. It is reported that he had only six years of piano training as a musical background. He began his formal musical studies at 22.

*Pictures from an Exhibition* was written in only a few weeks. A friend of Moussorgsky's, who had been a painter, died, and in tribute to his memory an exhibition of his paintings was held. Moussorgsky reproduced the pictures in his own series of musical paintings. He uses a theme (Promenade) which represents himself strolling through the gallery from one picture to another and thus connects the ten pictures together, creating a suite.

*Pictures from an Exhibition* is clearly a fine representation of Program Music. Program Music falls into three classifications: *Narrative* which tells a complete story; *descriptive* which portrays a mood, idea or story; and *imitative* which reproduces the exact sounds of animals or nature or things.

Moussorgsky's musical career brought him nothing but poverty and he soon became an alcoholic and died when only 42 years old. His music is still enjoyed today.

**Nikolai Rimsky-Korsakoff** (1844-1908) came from an aristocratic family. He had both musical and naval training. Korsakoff taught composition at St. Petersburg Conservatory and had a tremendous understanding and feel for the instruments of the orchestra. He was unequaled in the use of tone color for the orchestra.

It was Korsakoff who aided the other members of the Russian Five by editing and correcting many of their musical works.

One of his masterful programmatic works is *Scheherazade,* a symphonic suite. It is an adventurous tale of romance and comedy based on the *Tales of the Arabian Nights*. Korsakoff selected from these Tales certain ones for his symphonic suite. His new and exciting instrumental combinations and vivid timbre of orchestral instruments gave a striking, glittering musical picture.

Korsakoff wrote a book about himself called *My Musical Life* which reflects his spirit and his feelings.

The five Russians, although promoting their own musical heritage, were also influenced by earlier Germans and by some French schools of music.

### RECALL

1. In Russia five men sought to develop a Russian School of Music. They were _____ , _____, _____, _____ and _____.

2. The music of _____ and _____ is not widely known or performed.

3. Borodin is noted for his outstanding opera "_____ _____".

4. Program music falls into three classifications: narrative, _____ and _____.

5. What is the title of the program music Moussorgsky wrote in tribute to his artist friend? _____.

6. Rimsky-Korsakoff was unequalled in his use of _____ _____ for the orchestra.

7. One of Rimsky-Korsakoff's masterful programmatic works is "_____".

## PETER ILYICH TCHAIKOVSKY
### 1940-1893

Tchaikovsky was born in Votinsk, Russia. Although he was allowed to study piano, his father insisted that he also study law and sent him to the School of Jurisprudence. At nineteen he became a clerk at the Ministry of Justice. After this brief career, he seriously pursued the study of music and entered the St. Peterburg Conservatoire to study composition under Anton Rubinstein. After Tchaikovsky graduated in 1865, Rubinstein secured for him private pupils and a professorship at the Moscow Conservatory where he remained until he died.

Tchaikovsky was a very sentimental man who expressed himself in a very emotional manner. Having a wealthy widow as a financial backer, Tchaikovsky could spend his free time on nothing but composition.

His music is captivating and his melodies beautiful. He combines both mood and atmosphere with smooth unity of movement in his symphonic works. His most popular symphonic work is *Symphony No. 5 in E Minor, Opus 64.* His ballets are exciting and the *Nutcracker Suite* from the *Casse-Noisette* ballet, first performed in 1892 during the Christmas Season, is still performed in many countries. It is one of Tchaikovsky's most outstanding compositions.

### RECALL

1. Tchaikovsky entered the St. Petersburg Conservatoire to study composition under _____ _____.

2. His most popular ballet is the "_____ _____".

3. Tchaikovsky's most popular symphonic work is "_____".

## DIMITRI SHOSTAKOVICH
### 1906-

Dimitri Shostakovich's mother gave him his early musical training on the piano at the age of nine. He also studied piano and composition at the St. Petersburg Conservatoire with Nikolayev, Steinberg and Glazunov.

From 1919 to 1925, Shostakovich was a student at the Leningrad Conservatory. For his graduation composition he wrote his first symphony, *The Symphony in F Major, Opus 10.* Its premiere performance was on May 12, 1926 by the Leningrad Philharmonic Orchestra, with Nikolai Malko as conductor. Following its premiere performance, this symphony was programmed in Moscow, Berlin, Philadelphia and New York. This earned Shostakovich an international reputation although he was only twenty-three years old.

Shostakovich considered himself somewhat of a musical rebel. He felt his music reflected his beliefs in his country and their proletarian government.

Although his countrymen held him in high esteem, some of his music caused him to receive severe criticism from his government on several occasions. He fell out of favor with the government several times only to compose something new and find himself back in its good graces and still the foremost composer of music from Soviet Russia. He won the Stalin Prize five times as well as the International Sibelius Award and an Outstanding Award from the Austrian Republic. Shostakovich received the title of the "Hero of Socialist Labor"—the highest honor that can be bestowed on a citizen of Soviet Russia. He was the first musician to ever receive this award.

### RECALL

1. Dimitri Shostakovich's _____ gave him his early musical training.

2. For his graduation composition he wrote his first symphony, the "_____

_____ _____

_____, Opus 10, No. 1".

3. Shostakovich considered himself somewhat of a _____ _____.

# Czecheslovakia
### (Bohemia)

## BEDRICH SMETANA
### 1824-1884

Bedrich Smetana was a Bohemian composer who was also a fantastic pianist. In his compositions Smetana makes use of the rich folk music of his countrymen.

Smetana is most noted for his operas which were based on national subjects. His most famous is *The Bartered Bride,* a comic opera. His symphonic tone poem *The Moldau* also is a noted work. Smetana's nationalistic writing tendencies are most evident in his large cycle of symphonic poems in which he grouped *Vysehrael* and *The Moldau* along with four others and called them *My Fatherland* (Ma Vlast).

Smetana

# ANTONIN DVORAK
## 1841-1904

Antonin Dvorak was influenced by Smetana and also had a strong nationalistic musical style.

He was born near Prague and although his parents were poor, they believed in his musical ability and allowed him to study viola, violin, voice and organ. In 1874 Dvorak received the Austrian State Prize for his *Third Symphony in E-Flat*. This attracted Brahms' attention and he arranged an introduction to the German publisher Simrock.

Dvorak taught composition at the Prague Conservatoire for a brief time and in 1892 he was invited to New York to become the Director of the National Conservatory of Music. His stay in America, although short (Dvorak returned home in 1895), influenced his compositions. He did much to inspire and awaken the American people to the folk contributions of the Early Americans, and Blacks.

During his holidays in Spillville, Iowa, a mostly Bohemian town, Dvorak worked on his most famous Symphony, *From the New World*. This symphony is based on folk themes and folk-like themes of the Black Slaves and Bohemians.

Harry T. Burleigh attended the National Conservatory of Music and studied with Dvorak. He helped collect and notate some of the folk melodies. The "Largo" movement of the *New World Symphony* is based on the old Spiritual *In De Fold*. The melody is identical with the melody of the Spiritual. Another theme in G major clearly reminds the listener of the spiritual, *Swing Low, Sweet Chariot*.

During his time in America, Dvorak did not try to become an American citizen. But he did write his "Quartet in F, Op. 96" which is called *American*. When Dvorak returned home, he became Director of the Prague Conservatoire, a post he held until death in 1904.

## RECALL

1. In his compositions, Smetana made use of the rich _____ _____ of his countrymen.

2. His most famous opera is "_____ _____ _____".

3. Dvorak was influenced by _____.

4. "From the New World" is based on folk tunes of the _____ _____.

5. _____ _____ attended the National Conservatory of Music and studied Dvorak.

6. The music of Smetana and Dvorak was strongly _____.

antonin Dvořák

# Scandinavia
## EDVARD GRIEG
## 1843-1907

Edvard Grieg

The Norwegian composer, Edvard Grieg, found inspiration for his writings in the hills and streams, the rivers and mountains, and in all of the beautiful natural surroundings of his country.

Grieg had always been interested in music. His first lessons were from his mother (an amateur pianist) when he was six years old. He also tried to compose music at an early age.

He traveled to Germany in 1858 where he studied at the Leipzig Conservatoire until 1862. After meeting a group of Norwegian nationalist writers and composers in 1864, the nationalistic style of writing completely dominated his works.

He married his cousin, a singer, in 1867, and made several visits to Italy which were financed by state grants. While in Italy he had the good fortune of meeting Franz Liszt who admired Grieg greatly. Grieg devoted most of his time to composition. He frequently toured America and Europe as conductor, solo pianist or accompanist for his wife.

Grieg's *Concerto in A Minor—Opus 16* is the most popular piano concerto in music literature. Another of his outstanding works is his incidental music to Ibsen's *Peer Gynt Suite* (1876). His later works reflect even more expressions of nationalism as revealed in his *Norwegian Peasant Dances for Piano* written in 1902.

The death of his strongest nationalistic allies slowed his movement for creating a national school of composers. Yet, he maintained his spirit of nationalism until his death in Bergen in 1907.

## JAN SIBELIUS
## 1865-1957

Jan Sibelius, even as a child in Finland, showed musical talent. His family, however, wanted him to become a lawyer. He entered the University of Helsingfors to study law and at the same time began to take violin lessons at the Conservatory. After a year he was given permission to pursue the career of music. He went to Berlin and Vienna to study and returned to his home country in 1893.

Sibelius' great talent was recognized and appreciated by the government and he was granted a life pension in 1897. This enabled him to spend all of his time writing music. For thirty years he composed what he wished with the understanding and appreciation of his countrymen.

He was basically a symphonic composer. His most popular composition is *Finlandia*, a symphonic poem. It is a symbol of Finland's national spirit and the anthem of independence. At the time it was composed, Finland was dominated or ruled by Russia. Although Sibelius completed this work in 1899, it was not allowed to he heard until 1905.

Jan Sibelius

## RECALL

1. Grieg's first lessons were from his mother (an amateur pianist) when he was _____ years old.
2. After meeting a group of Norweigian nationalist writers and composers in 1864, the _____ style of writing completely dominated his work.
3. What work by Grieg is the most popular piano concerto in all music literature? _____.
4. Jan Sibelius studied law and at the same time began to take _____ lessons.
5. His great talent was recognized and appreciated by the government and he was granted a _____ _____ in 1897.
6. His most popular composition, a symphonic poem, is "_____".

# Brazil

## HEITOR VILLA-LOBOS
## 1887-1959

Heitor Villa-Lobos, a Brazilian composer, did much to improve music education and make known the folk heritage of his native countrymen.

Villa-Lobos was born in Rio de Janeiro. He had only a limited education because he had to earn his own way at an early age. He worked in restaurants, cafes and theatres, where he heard the popular songs of his people. He attended the National Institute of Music in Rio de Janeiro; however, the scheduled curriculum seemed stifling to him. He left the school and continued to gather his musical knowledge through his own experiences.

About 1916 he married a young conservatory-trained pianist and settled in his home city. Artur Rubenstein heard some of Villa-Lobos' works and encouraged him to obtain financial support from the government in order to study abroad.

Lobos obtained a grant and went to Paris to study for four years. When he returned to his native country, he first became the Director of Musical Education in Sao Paulo and then in Rio de Janeiro.

He created several musically innovative methods for teaching children: He created enthusiastic interest in singing by making great use of native folk songs for Children to sing in choruses; and he developed a system which taught children who could not read music to sing classical songs. This was done by using hand signals.

Lobos, being an excellent conductor, attracted much attention to the music of his country and was very definitely a nationalistic composer.

He continued writing until his death in 1959 and his works number upwards of two thousand. His music is descriptive, narrative and imitative with a rich and pleasing harmonic content. It is colorful, alive and full of the rhythmic ferver of the Brazilian people. His *Danses Africanas* (African Dances), a group of three dances for orchestra, and his *Amazonas,* a tone poem for orchestra, make use of Brazilian rhythms and folk legends.

Villa-Lobos toured the United States three times—first in 1944, and again in 1947 and 1957.

## RECALL

1. Heitor Villa-Lobos, a Brazilian composer, did much to improve _____ education

and make known the folk heritage of his own country.

2. _____ _____ heard some of his works and encouraged him to obtain financial support from the government.

3. He created several musically innovative methods for teaching _____.

4. Villa-Lobos' music is _____, _____ and imitative with a rich and pleasing harmonic content.

# England

## RALPH VAUGH WILLIAMS
## 1872-1958

Vaughan Williams was a composer devoted to the development of the folk heritage of his country, England. His works are full of rich melodies and harmonies which make the listener aware of the fact that the composer is of the 20th century. Dissonance is not absent but its presence is felt along with the traditional harmonies in a manner that blends very well and enhances the text until one feels the nationalistic flavor.

Williams' works range from symphonies to sacred works and operas. He has encouraged other composers to promote nationalistic music. His symphonies, *London, Sea* and *Pastoral* are musical blends of both the old and the new.

## RECALL

1. Ralph Vaughan Williams was a composer devoted to the development of the folk heritage of his country, _____.
2. His works are full of rich _____ and _____.
3. He has encouraged other composers to promote _____ music.

## SIR WILLIAM WALTON
## 1902-

Sir William Walton's father was a church choir director. Walton's music lessons started when he was five. He attended the Christ Church Cathedral Choir School at Oxford and went directly to Christ Church in 1918 at the early age of 16.

Walton was influenced by the romantic school of music. His compositions include film music, ballets, background music for movies, operas and his famous oratorio, *Belshazzai's Feast* (1931). This work features baritone solo, orchestra and chorus. It is an impressive and powerful work.

Oxford University gave him an honorary doctorate in music. He was knighted in 1951 and composed a Te Deum for the Coronation of Queen Elizabeth in 1954.
He came to the United States on tour in 1838 as guest conductor of his *Crown Imperial Coronation March.*

## RECALL

1. Sir William Walton is an _____ composer.

2. Walton's music lessons started when he was _____.

3. What is the title of his famous oratorio?
_____

## BENJAMIN BRITTEN
## 1913-1976

Benjamin Britten was an important English composer. He believed that the composer should be a part of the community and have direct contact with its people. He also felt that the composer should use any devices and techniques necessary to express his ideas and emotions in an understandable manner.

Britten's writings, therefore, do not fall into any one school of expression. Each composition reflects the materials, techniques, style and emotions necessary for that particular composition. Britten has been influenced to some degree by Schoenberg and Mahler.

Britten was a prolific writer even at an early age. He began writing at the age of five and at seven began playing the piano. By nine, he had composed an oratorio and a string quartet and by fourteen, quartets, piano sonatas, many songs and a symphony. He was an associate at the Royal College of Music because of his piano playing and the Ernest Farrar Prize was awarded him.

Britten visited America briefly but returned to his home in 1942.

One of his major works is the opera, *Peter Grimes.* He was commissioned to write this opera by the Koussevitzky Music Foundation. This opera established Britten as one of England's great Composers.

Britten has received honorary doctorates from the University of Belfast (1954) and Cambridge (1959). He was the only composer requested to write an opera for a coronation in England (June 8, 1953). He also founded and directed the English Opera Group and the annual Aldeburgh Festival.

## RECALL

1. Benjamin Britten is an important _____ composer.
2. Britten's writings do _____ fall into any school of expression.
3. He has been influenced to some degree by _____ and Mahler.
4. One of his major works is "_____ _____".

# Hungary
## BELA BARTÓK
## 1881-1945

Bela Bartók, along with Kodaly, gathered and analyzed hundreds of authentic Hungarian folk songs and melodies. They attempted to find a way other composers could incorporate this Hungarian folklore into their music.

Bartók felt that in order to write in the folk idiom of a country, one must be completely immersed in its folk traditions and understand and withdraw only the means of musical expression before transforming it to his own musical ideas.

Bartók influenced many composers and is as important to the musical world as Schoenberg and Stravinsky. His works are both complex and easy. He wrote many studies for the piano. His *Mikrokosmos* (Little World) studies, written for his son Peter, took eleven years and include 153 pieces. All aspects of keyboard style, from simple to complex, are included in the set. It is a book of devices used by 20th century composers.

Bartók's works range from orchestral pieces to songs. They show exceptional musical understanding, concept and skills and combine old and new musical devices and techniques with nationalistic fervor.

## ZOLTAN KODALY
## 1882-1967

The Hungarian composer, Zoltan Kodaly, worked along with Bartók to gather the folk songs of the Hungarian people. Kodaly is known for his many choral works. He created many rhapsodies and became known throughout the world for creating rhapsodies using folk ingredients. He wrote many fine choral works, some chamber music, songs, piano music and works for organ. The best known of his works is the *Hary Janos Suite* written in 1926. This suite relates the imaginary facts of a soldier's past and is taken from the opera. An interesting folk tale is the Hungarian belief or superstition that if a person sneezes while telling a story, the sneeze proves the story us true. Kodaly begins his composition by allowing the entire orchestra to sneeze in concert. The suite is divided into six sections.

## RECALL

1. _____ and Kodaly gathered and analyzed hundreds of authentic Hungarian folk songs and melodies.
2. Bartók's works are both _____ and easy.
3. His "_____" studies written for his son Peter took eleven years and included 153 pieces.
4. Kodaly was a _____ composer.
5. Zoltan Kodaly worked along with _____ to gather the folk songs of the Hungarian people.
6. Kodaly's best known work is the "_____ _____ Suite".

# Germany

## CARL ORFF
## 1895-

The works of Carl Orff can be placed into three categories: cantatas—which use some action and optional dance; instructional compositions—five volumes of music for children explaining his new approaches, techniques and experiences in and with contemporary music education for the young student; and operas and plays—in which Orff usually makes use of fairy tales.

Orff does not refer to his works as operas and is an exponent of symbolic theatre. His most famous work is *Carmina Burana,* a cantata for choir, soloists and orchestra. Orff's music, though contemporary, is plain enough to be appreciated by the average listener.

# The Expressionist School of Music
# 1900-

## ARNOLD SCHOENBERG
## 1874-1951

It was Arnold Schoenberg who charted the path for the *Expressionist* School of music. The Expressionist movement represents a breakaway from the French

Arnold Schoenberg

Impressionistic School. It tries to express the inner reality—the subconscious. Schoenberg, born in Vienna, began his study of music when he was eight. The violin was his first instrument. He began to compose, to some degree, when he was twelve. His early works reflect the influence of the post-Romantic period and it was not until about 1924 that he developed his completely new approach to writing music that is reflected in his use of "twelve tone technique".

The twelve tone technique uses 12 selected tones of the chromatic scale arranged in a fixed tone row (order). The tones may be arranged in a melodic manner, providing they are not repeated until all tones are used. There are no dominant tones—all tones are of equal significance. The composer then builds his composition on a tone row. The entire composition consists of a restatement of the series in various formations. For example: vertical, horizontal, retrograde (melody written backwards) and inverted.

Schoenberg's first composition based solely on this technique was the *Suite for Piano, Opus 25.* From 1920-1949 Schoenberg's music reflected a cold, mathematical approach which lacked feeling. The interesting new

technique and new creative inventiveness were evident but the weird, dissonant, seemingly unorganized combinations of tones made it difficult for the listener to understand and accept.

After 1940, Schoenberg resorted to the use of the 12 tone system, sometimes combined with conventional techniques and sometimes with romanticism.

Schoenberg came to America in 1933 after he had been ousted by the Nazis. His new musical compositions and Jewish heritage served to infuriate them. He taught at three colleges: the Malkin School of Music in Boston, the University of Southern California and the University of California at Los Angeles. He lived in Brentwood, California, when he died.

## ALBAN BERG
## 1885-1935

Alban Berg revealed a great deal of emotion in his use of the 12 tone technique. Berg's most famous work is his opera, *Wozzeck* (the story of man's inhumanity to man). In this opera, Berg made use of atonality (a lack of key) identification), the 12 tone technique and traditional harmony.

## ANTON WEBERN
## 1883-1945

Anton Webern was born in Vienna. His music made use solely of the 12 tone system and all of its techniques. Webern completely disregarded traditional techniques. He does use carefully inserted periods of silence, as an important part of a composition and emphasizes canons. Otherwise, there is little repetition and his compositions are very short.

His Expressionist practices and style of writing reflect a complete break with traditional techniques and introduce a pure form of Expressionism which fully uses serialism (12 tone technique).

The three composers, Schoenberg, Berg and Webern, paved the way for a new school of music (Expressionism) which influenced a generation of new composers.

## RECALL

1. It was _____ _____
   who charted the path for the Expressionist
   School of Music.
2. The twelve tone technique used the 12 tones of
   the _____ scale arranged in a fixed
   row (order). There are no _____
   tones.
3. Alban Berg's most famous work is the opera
   "_____".
4. Anton Webern's music made use solely of the
   _____ _____ system
   and all of its techniques.

# MODERN AMERICA

## Jazz
## From 1900

# MODERN AMERICA
# JAZZ
# From 1900

## Before the Civil War

When you think about the birth of jazz you usually think of the South and New Orleans. This new music style really burst into full bloom in the early 1900's, although its roots began with early slave music.

The city of New Orleans had several unique factors which give a clear picture of the elements contributing to the development of jazz: 1) It was a French and later a Spanish settlement where festive occasions were traditional and frequent; 2) It was the meeting point of three major cultures—the French, Spanish and Anglo-Saxon, and 3) It had a divided Black community—the 'Uptown Blacks' and the 'Downtown Blacks.'

The 'Uptown Blacks' were given no educational opportunities because it was feared that their education might cause insurrection. They also had no citizenship rights and were not allowed to marry. They worked very long hours with very little rest.

Both the Spanish and the French governments had an official state religion and even the slaves were expected to follow these religious practices although contrary to their African beliefs. This caused the 'Uptown Blacks' to hold secret meetings in order to practice their own religion. It was from their own religious ceremonies that they received any comfort or release of tension from the strain under which they were living. Some slaves' religious ceremonies were accompanied by body movements and the use of some home made instruments.

The slaves insisted on holding religious celebrations regardless of threats and punishments by slave owners. These practices and celebrations included customs not understood by the Spanish, French or 'Downtown Blacks' but eventually become a vital part of New Orleans life. On Saturday and Sunday nights Congo Square was opened to the slaves for their ceremonies and it soon became a great tourist attraction.

The other segment of the Black community known as The 'Downtown Blacks' were called Creoles. In New Orleans, any Black person who could prove at least one drop of French or Spanish blood was treated as a 'freed Black' citizen with full rights of citizenship: he could work for pay, own his own home or business and pursue an education.

Many Creoles attended colleges not only in the United States but also in Europe. To many, this afforded an excellent opportunitiy to obtain a music education. They enjoyed events in concert halls, opera houses and festive occasions where European music was dominant. To a large number of Creoles, the music to which they were exposed and the musical training available was a symbol of prestige. Music often became an avocation. To a lesser number of Creoles, music was a serious study leading to a full-time musical career.

## After the Civil War

After the Civil War, the Creoles (Downtown Blacks) no longer enjoyed the liberty of being first-class citizens. They were now treated the same as 'Uptown Blacks.' The Emancipation Proclamation and the War left bitter wounds. Jobs were few and all Blacks were now in competition with Whites.

The influence of the French who used music at every festive occasion remained. Bands began to be used for parades, parties, riverboat excursions, funerals, dances, weddings and religious functions. Although the demand for bands was great, the competition was keen.

'Uptown Blacks' found used European instruments left behind by Confederate and Union demobilized military bands. They also obtained instruments from pawn shops, homes and other places. 'Downtown Blacks,' for the most part, had been exposed to European instruments and many still owned their own instruments.

Most of the 'Uptown Blacks' were self-taught. Their lack of experience and formal musical training on European instruments developed innovative methods of playing. They used every instrument as if playing a solo. Not being able to read music and often having no score to play from even if they could, they skillfully imitated and improvised, to the smallest detail, exactly what they heard. These band members knew no limitations where the range of their instruments was concerned. Their ability to play almost anything they heard, from classical music to jazz, without sheet music made it difficult to know who could and who couldn't read music.

The 'Downtown Black' musicians were very structured musically. Most could read music and they played music within the traditions of the European schools. Although they were well-trained, few could improvise. Their musical avocation of before the war was now to become, in many cases, their vocation.

The coming together of 'Downtown' and 'Uptown Blacks' created an instinctively musical community. The Creoles made a formal, structured musical contribution playing European music and using European techniques and skills. The 'Uptown Blacks' contributed an informal, unstructured, inventive means of playing music based on new technical skills. Performers were encouraged to exercise the freedom to use their instruments to the fullest capacity. On the spot improvising or creating was important and impressive. This was a new technique and sound which included the use of new harmony, musical idioms, vocabulary and virtuosity. It also demanded a unique way of 'razzing' around the music using African syncopated rhythms.

This music was taken from folk sources: work songs, spirituals, chants, dance music, hollers, shouts, sea chanteys, field songs, blues and cermonial music. This folk heritage, combined with the European structured music background of the Creole, gave rise to a new American sound and style of music called Jazz.

Jazz may be defined as an American style of playing music where a given theme or melody is stated. This is followed by a democratic sequence of alternately allowing each performer in the ensemble the opportunity to razz, ridicule, liven-up, tease, expand, contract, mourn, lament or play around with the given theme or melody (improvise). Next, there usually is a return to the given theme or melody by the ensemble and an ending (sign out, tag, close out or coda).

## RECALL

1. When you think about the birth of Jazz, you usually think about the South and _____ _____.

2. New Orleans was the meeting point of three major cultures: the _____ , _____ and _____.

3. It had a Black community divided into the _____ _____ and the _____ _____.

4. The _____ _____ were slaves and had no educational opportunities.

5. The _____ _____ or Creoles attended colleges which afforded them the opportunities to obtain a _____.

6. After the Civil War, the _____

_____ and the _____ _____ were treated the same.

7. The _____ _____ musicians were self-taught and were _____ to read music.

8. The _____ _____ musicians were very structured musically and _____ to read music.

9. Performers were encouraged to use their instruments to their _____ capacity.

10. Folk heritage, combined with the European structured music background of the Creole, gave rise to a new American sound and style of music called _____.

11. Write your definition of Jazz: _____ _____

# Ragtime

Ragtime can be described as a type of piano Jazz. The left hands maintains a definite-exacting rhythm while the right hand syncopates the melody (accents the weak beats of the measure).

This kind of playing was one of the earliest jazz styles. Unlike the blues form which is personal, sad and usually needs a singer, ragtime music is lively, vibrant, melodic and fun-type music, usually using only the piano.

After the emergence of ragtime music, it quickly swept through the United States and eventually the world. Fantastic 'rag' rhythms had been developing in Joel Walker Sweeney's guitar playing style. The complicated rhythms of the Cake Walk (a dance created by the slaves and used in early Minstrel Shows) were an early beginning of ragtime; after the Emancipation Proclamation in 1863, the freed Blacks played the instruments in exciting new styles, techniques and rhythms bordering on ragtime.

Scott Joplin (1868-1917), who is called the 'Master of Ragtime' and sometimes 'King' or 'Father' of Ragtime, is noted for his famous ragtime compositions. *Maple Leaf Rag* is one of his most famous. Joplin's ragtime playing was classic in style yet his compositions were both classical and popular. They demanded independent control of the different rhythms in each hand which combined to create a single multi-rhythmic composition. His works were, in many ways, as difficult as any of the European compositions by the great masters.

Joplin wrote not only ragtime piano music but also ragtime operas. *Tremonisha*, published in 1911, enjoyed a 1976 revival on Broadway. Joplin originally worked hard to produce this opera and it was first performed in concert style without costuming or scenery with the composer at the piano. It was not, however, successful during his lifetime. Another of Joplin's ragtime operas *A Guest in the House*, was also performed once in concert style.

The continuous sale of ragtime music by the popular sheet music publishers soon led to the creation of an artificial commercial ragtime sound. This led to the waning of the Ragtime Era just prior to the beginning of the classic Blues era.

Scott Joplin

The fact that most Black composers were not recognized in our early music history books accounts for their absence in later classifications. Like many of history's great composers, it is unfortunate that Scott Joplin's contribution has been acknowledged so late.

Other ragtime composers that should be remembered are Eubie Blake (1883-    ), Tom Turpin (1873-1922) and Ferdinand Joseph "Jelly Roll" Morton (1885-1941). In 1897, Turpin, who composed *Harlem Rag*, was the first to have a ragtime composition published and thus began the ragtime craze. Composers James P. Johnson (1891-1955) and Thomas "Fats" Waller (1904-1943) were also known for their ragtime playing. Two White ragtime composers that are remembered are Charles L. Johnson (1876-1950) and Joseph F. Lamb (1887-1960).

1. You could describe ragtime as a type of _____ _____ .

2. The left hand maintains a _____ _____ rhythm while the right hand _____ the melody.

3. _____ _____ is called the Master of Ragtime.

4. His compositions were both _____ and _____ .

5. "_____ _____ _____" is one of his most famous ragtime compositions.

6. Three other ragtime composers are: _____ , _____ and _____ .

## JAMES P. JOHNSON
## 1891-1955

James P. Johnson was not only one of the great ragtime composers, but also made an equal contribution to piano style and technique. He developed 'stride piano' (heavy left hand). Johnson made many piano rolls for the player pianos that were so popular at the turn of the century.

He was a trained musician who accompanied Ethel Waters, Mamie Smith and Bessie Smith. He wrote over thirty compositions including a symphonic suite on *St. Louis Blues*; two ballets — **Manhattan Street Scene** and *Sefronia's Dream*; two operettas — *Kitchen Opera* and *The Husband*; and a folk opera, *De Organizer*.

Johnson died in New York on November 17, 1955.

1. James P. Johnson was only one of the great _____ composers but also made an equal contribution to piano style and technique.

2. He developed 'stride piano' which means a _____ _____ _____ .

# Styles of Jazz

Early New Orleans style Jazz (sometimes called ragtime or Creole music) featured such outstanding jazz performers as "Buddy" Bolden on cornet, "Jelly Roll" Morton on piano and "King" Oliver on trumpet.

Charles "Buddy" Bolden (1868-1931) was certainly one of the first jazz artists of great magnitude. He played the cornet and trumpet and organized his own band. Although most of his musicians could not read music, they were still superb performers. Once they heard something, they could immediately reproduce it.

"Buddy" Bolden's band had a rough, forceful sound. They improvised using the African musical trait known as 'call and response.' That means the instruments imitated a leader when responding. His band produced an ensemble effect. The rhythm section kept a steady beat. The Bolden band instrumentation included a cornet, the lead instrument which played melody or simple variations on the melody; the clarinet, which played its own counter-melody between the notes of the cornet and in response to it; the trombone, which filled in the bass harmonies, also playing its own melody in reponse to the cornet lead; and the string bass, which played a steady backup rhythm.

Bolden's band played ragtime, polkas (dances in 2/2 time), quadrilles (Creole march tunes) and blues. Many bands were to follow his style of playing as well as his instrumentation. He could be considered the father of the New Orleans style of Jazz playing.

It must be remembered that the early New Orleans Jazzmen were usually working in other occupations. They were men skilled at various crafts ranging from painters to engravers and some owned their own businesses. They played Jazz on a part-time basis.

# Storyville
# 1897-1917

A section of New Orleans became known as Storyville. This was the area where full time entertainment became a business. It required the hiring of musicians who could play all night long.

The solo pianist in the ensemble soon emerged as the sole performer because it was easier and less expensive to hire one man to work long hours than an entire group. These pianists were called 'professors.' Their working hours were incredibly long. Among them are remembered "Jelly Roll" Morton and Tony Jackson.

Bands then began to advertise more and used highly decorated wagons telling where and when they would be playing. The entire band played on the wagon as it toured. If one wagon of band members met another wagon of band members, they engaged in a contest to see which band could out-play the other. The term for these unplanned contests was 'craving' or sometimes, 'cutting.' Large crowds of people often followed or walked right alongside the bands.

Aspiring young musicians often organized their own

bands and played on the streets outside businesses. The instruments they used were unusual: cowbells, clotheslines for strings, bass fiddles cut from sugar barrels and old kettles and long gas piping. They were called 'spasm' bands and were frequently training grounds for a lot of jazz musicians.

Louis "Satchmo" Armstrong (1900-1971) was a 'spasm' band member who began his career playing on a guitar made from a cigar box.

Often these band members took odd names such as 'Stale Bread Chinee' and 'Slew Foot Pete'. Stale Bread Chinee and Slew Foot Pete and others were young White musicians ranging in age from twelve to fifteen, who had organized a band. Whites from the slum areas of New Orleans also contributed to New Orleans Jazz. The most outstanding was Papa Jack Laine. He changed the fast tempo of the Black style of Jazz to a slower tempo. This was to become the new rhythm for Dixieland Jazz. Many White musicians in New Orleans worked with Papa Jude Laines' bands.

New Orleans was not the only place where Jazz was being played in those days nor was the New Orlean's style of playing Jazz the only style. However, this Jazz style was spread by the musicians working in circuses, vaudeville, wild west and minstrel shows and by some traveling bands used on river boat excursions. From the early 1900's until about 1917, Jazz spread north becoming very popular and indicating a migration by country Blacks into the cities. Like the early spiritual, Jazz became the new representative medium of expression for Blacks. Each section or region of the country had its own style.

The influx of drugs and crime into Storyville about 1897 created a change for Jazz musicians and a relocation process. When Storyville closed in 1917 the big migration gained momentum. By the 1920's the cities of New York, Kansas City and Chicago had become great Jazz centers. Few of the early bands used musical scores and most early Dixieland bands never recorded.

The early Dixieland marching bands led to the development of the 'regular' bands. Dixieland marching bands accompanied funeral processions. After the funeral, they began to play very lively music in order to change the mood and help the families forget their sadness. They 'razzed' around the melodies.

New Orleans (or early Dixieland) music may be described as follows: A polyphonic style Jazz in which the trumpet or cornet states the melody, then decorates or departs from the melody according to the player's feeling; at the same time, the clarinet 'razzes' around with a counter melody as sort of an answer to the cornet or trumpet (obligato type); the trombone plays around with the harmony below the melody; the rhythm section, which may include drums, string bass, guitar or piano, tuba, banjo, or drum keeps the simple rhythmic beat usually 4/4.

The musical pattern of the Dixieland Band was
   A. Ensemble plays
   B. Solos play
   C. Ensemble plays
and improvisations were allowed during solos and ensembles.

You can visit Storyville in New Orleans to this day. This district reverberates with the sound of jazz every night. Just look for the "French Quarter."

## RECALL

1. _____ _____ was one of the first jazz artists of great magnitude.
2. His band had a coarse, forceful sound and improvised using the African musical trait known as _____ _____ _____.
3. A section of New Orleans became known as _____.
4. The _____ _____ in the ensemble emerged as the leader.
5. Louis Armstrong was a _____ band member.

6. _____ _____ _____ changed the fast tempo of the Black style of jazz to a slower tempo.
7. Like the early spiritual, _____ became the new representative medium of expression for Blacks.
8. Few of the early bands used _____ _____.
9. New Orleans (or early Dixieland) music may be described as a _____ style jazz.
10. Storyville is now called the _____ _____.

## LOUIS "SATCHMO" ARMSTRONG
## 1900-1971

The man with the golden trumpet, often referred to as 'The Ambassador of Jazz', is Louis "Satchmo" Armstrong. Born in New Orleans, "Satchmo" became a member of a spasm band. These bands performed on the street and constructed their own instruments.

He was a composer, author and conductor and without a doubt, the most important single performer on the Jazz scene. He was a singer, trumpet player and an entertainer. One can hardly read the history of jazz without finding him appearing with or playing for most of the outstanding

artists all the way from "Ma" Rainey to Bessie Smith and "King" Oliver's Band.

"Satchmo" remained, regardless of the changing styles of Jazz, the world's best known representative of this medium. His early techniques on the trumpet were an innovation.

He appeared in several movies and on radio and television shows. Touring the world, he was hailed by leaders, musicians and people everywhere as the greatest individualistic trumpet player-performer to have lived. His

Louis Armstrong

technique was so exceptional that it seemed he was born with the trumpet.

Louis Armstrong's musical understanding and love of the theatre and the people made him a truly great ambassador of jazz music.

### RECALL

1. Louis Armstrong became a member of a _____ band.

2. He was a singer, _____ player and entertainer.

3. Armstrong is often called the _____ of Jazz.

# Chicago Dixieland

The great migration from New Orleans to other large cities started in 1917. This was somewhat due to the closing of jazz centers in New Orleans by Federal officers because of an influx of drugs and crime.

Benny Goodman

Chicago then became one of the leading jazz centers in the country. The Jazz musicians attracted to Chicago were destined to become famous. Among them were Louis "Satchmo" Armstrong (1900-1971), Earl "Fatha" Hines (1905-    ), Sidney Bechet, "Jelly Roll" Morton (1885-1941), Johnny Dodds and the "Original Dixieland Jazz Band" (a White group).

At thirty-fifth and State Streets, the old Pekin Theatre became Chicago's Jazz headquarters. Many professionals and hopeful amateurs received their inspiration from listening to these great artists on the South side of Chicago. The now famous King of Swing—Benny Goodman (1909-    ), Gene Krupa (1909-1973) and "Muggsy" Spanier were then Austin High School students who frequented the Pekin Theatre. Other popular jazz spots were the Grand Theatre, the Vendome Theatre, the Club De Lisa (where Joe Williams, the jazz singer, was discovered) and countless cabarets located all over the city. Many outstanding pianists were influenced by the contribution of "Fatha" Hines, one of the best jazz pianists, who played Chicago at the time.

Chicago Dixieland Music took on big city complexities: the simple rhythm of New Orleans (4/4) was replaced with the complex, syncopated rhythms used in ragtime; the guitar was frequently substituted for the banjo; and the tenor saxophone was added. The elements of tension in the music became very intense. Beginnings and endings took on more complex structures and elaborate introductions were added. Endings expanded into what seemed almost like codas and codettas (short selections of additional musical ideas). It seemed to be a natural evolution because, in this era there were more well-trained and skillful instrumentalists available.

### RECALL

1. _____ became one of the leading jazz centers in the country.

2. Name two jazz musicians who have become famous that were attracted to Chicago: _____ and _____.

3. _____ _____,
   _____ _____ and
   _____ _____ were
   Austin High School students who frequented the
   Pekin Theatre.

4. Earl '_____' _____ was

one of the best jazz pianists who played Chicago
at that time.

5. Chicago _____ _____
   took on city complexities.

6. In this era there were more _____
   _____ and skillful instrumentalists
   available.

# Boogie Woogie
# 1930-1940

'Boogie-Woogie' can be described as a pianistic Jazz style. The music expresses little sentiment but rather a technical rhythmic-musical relationship. Boogie Woogie music origins can be traced far south to the Texas lumber camps. Its style was developing as early as 1918.

Many pianists in the South were migratory workers. They were very competitive and were constantly trying to better their style of playing. As a result, the bass of Boogie Woogie music simply has repeated patterns. One could say that the bass 'walks' around; in fact, it was called 'walking bass', a sort of ostinato effect. The right hand plays a melody and sometimes melodic variations. Boogie Woogie follows the twelve bar 'blues' pattern. The difference is that the left hand sort of walks through the

removed the top of the piano in order to obtain more sound and volume. This music is thrilling and creates a lot of excitement.

Boogie-Woogie music was used frequently at house-rent parties on the South side of Chicago where rents were relatively high. These were parties where one paid at the door to enter and then paid for food and drinks. Entertainment was provided by Boogie Woogie pianists. This helped the host of the house party to pay his rent.

The only way to learn to play Boogie Woogie was by watching and listening. The social connotations among Blacks of the time about Boogie Woogie music was that it was a lower class music and not for respectable people. But, Boogie Woogie was a true outgrowth of the 'Blues' style. Among its outstanding contributors and performers were pianists Pepe Johnson, Jimmy Yancey, Meade Lux Lewis, Clarence "Pine Top" Smith, Hazel Scott, called "Queen of Boogie-

Hazel Scott

Dorothy Donegan

repeated bass pattern using the chords of the twelve bar 'Blues'. The right hand plays the melody or various improvisations on the harmony indicated by the bass pattern. The rhythm is lively and rapid.

During the early '30's, Boogie Woogie pianists often

Woogie Pianists" and Dorothy Donnegan. The Boogie-Woogie pianist served to replace the more expensive bands after the depression.

1. Boogie Woogie can be described as a _____ jazz style.

2. The bass of Boogie Woogie music simply has _____ _____ in the left hand.

3. The _____ _____ plays the meldoy or variations.
4. Boogie Woogie follows the _____ _____ blues pattern.
5. The only way to learn to play Boogie Woogie was by _____ and _____.

# Swing Era
# 1932-1942

Students of Chicago Jazz were to lead America into the era of 'Swing' music. About the time of the Swing era, dancing had become very popular and swing music best reflected the dancing needs of the people.

This was the day of the big bands playing musical arrangements. Unlike Dixieland, Swing was carefully written out with only a few improvised solos. Swing band arrangements, for big bands up to 24 pieces, were usually homophonic melodies (just one melody) supported by chords. The 4/4 meter was dominant.

A major factor in swing music was that the band or orchestra reflected mostly the musical ideas of one composer or arranger. Even the improvised sections were restrained. This was very unlike the traditional Jazz band or Jazz orchestra compositions and arrangements that allowed any member to improvise within the framework of the music.

Benny Goodman earned the reputation of the 'King of Swing'. As a high school student at Austin High in Chicago, Goodman frequently visited the famous old Pekin Theatre on 35th and State Streets where outstanding Black musicians of the time played.

An associate of Benny Goodman was James "Fletcher" Henderson (1897-1952), one of the world's great Swing composers and arrangers. Henderson prepared over 800 arrangements for Benny Goodman. His *Christopher Columbus* made the Hit Parade. Henderson received many awards for his outstanding talent and his genius may well be responsible for what we now refer to as the Swing Era. Some feel that he could be credited with starting the big band movement.

Benny Goodman's music was not only especially good for dancing, but his recordings were among the first to be successfully promoted by disc jockeys. It would also be fair to say that the use of his music increased the popularity of the disc jockey programs. The disc jockey soon became so important that he could make or break a record or an artist.

William "Count" Basie (1904-    ) was born in Red Bank, New Jersey but became active in jazz in Kansas City, Missouri. Another giant of the Swing Era, he was known as the 'Impressario of the Blues'. His music was modern in approach and was the bridge from the Swing Era to 'Cool Jazz' and 'Bop'. The Basie Band had a deeper, more penetrating beat, and his *One O'Clock Jump* hit the million mark in sales. The Count's piano playing style gave less emphasis to the left hand, leaving the heavy basic beat to the bass player. He frequently opened with a bass fiddle solo. His saxophone player, Lester Young, reflected the direction in which Count Basie was headed—to that of a cool style Jazz. Like Wagner's introduction of the leitmotiv (a theme used to identify a particular character) in opera, Count Basie introduced the unison phrase played alternately by the reed and the brass sections of the band called the head riff. These riffs were often complicated and almost developed into a polyphonic composition. This use of riffs as the opening melody became an outstanding feature of Kansas City big bands.

Big bands remained in the foreground for over ten years. Among the famous big bands were Duke Ellington, Cab Calloway, Louis Armstrong, Lionel Hampton, Chick Webb, Guy Lombardo, Kay Kayser, Fletcher-Henderson, Count Basie, Benny Goodman, Jimmie Lunceford, Glen Miller, Tommy Dorsey, Woody Herman (1913-    ) Coleman Hawkins (1904-1969), and Artie Shaw. The big bands saw the development of great orchestral arrangers and conductors like Gerald Wilson who worked with Jimmie Lunceford and recorded several works with his own orchestra; Cy Oliver who worked with Jimmie Lunceford and Tommy Dorsey; and Charlie Barnett who recorded the ideas and style of Count Basie.

1. Swing band arrangements for big bands up to 24 pieces were usually _____ melodies supported by chords.
2. The _____ meter was dominant.
3. A major factor in swing music was that the band or orchestra reflected mostly the musical ideas of _____ composer or arranger.
4. _____ earned the reputation of the 'King of Swing'.
5. Fletcher _____ prepared over 800 arrangements for Benny Goodman!
6. Benny Goodman's music was not only especially good for dancing, but his recordings were among the first to be successfully promoted by _____ jockeys.
7. Count Basie introduced the unison phrase played alternately by the reed and brass sections of the band called the _____ _____.
8. The Swing Era came to a close around _____.

# Pop Music 1930-1954

'Pop' music is a title used to describe commercially composed music. Pop music was constantly played for the entire country on radio, television and in the movies from the end of the Classical Blues Era (1929-1930) until about 1954. Music from various sources of American styles competed for radio's "Hit Parade" which was the measuring rod, at that time, for the choice of the most popular songs. The common forms ranged from the 32-bar song (standard type) which sometimes came from the musical theater or the movies; country and western type ballads (both folk and commercial); serious Pop music which included all forms of Jazz and Jazz symphonic styles; and Rhythm and Blues (seldom heard on the Hit Parade).

Each Pop artist had a stylized vocal sound and his own *national audience. The Hit Parade and radio programs* determined the hits and the biggest stars. Accompaniments usually included a full orchestra and the music was made for easy listening. Pop music of the time was geared to the adults. It expressed a sort of make-believe world where many of life's real problems were seldom sung about.

Some of the Pop singers were Doris Day, Eddie Fischer, Perry Como, Frankie Laine, Judy Garland, Bing Crosby, Billy Eckstein, Sara Vaughn, Kate Smith, Jo Stafford, Ella Fitzgerald, Patti Page, Margaret Whiting, Anita O'Day, Pearl Bailey, Nat "King" Cole (1917-1965),

Joe Williams, Dinah Shore, Frank Sinatra and Sophie Tucker. Some of their hits were *This Love of Mine, I Wish I Didn't Love You So, There! I've Said It Again, Open the Door, Richard, The Alphabet Song, Mona Lisa, The White Cliffs of Dover, Besame Mucho (Kiss Me Much), Be Careful, It's My Heart, Goodnight, Irene, If I Knew You Were Coming Id'a Baked a Cake, My Heart Cries For You, Tennessee Waltz, Glow-Worm, Your Cheatin' Heart* and *The Doggie in the Window.*

There were also many popular groups such as the Ink Spots, the Andrew Sisters, the McGuire Sisters, the Mills Brothers, Les Paul and Mary Ford and the Golden Gate Quartet.

Popular artists who were instrumental musicians included Erroll Garner, Carmen Cavallaro, Harry James, Art Tatum, Lionel Hampton, Dorothy Donegan and Hazel Scott.

Popular orchestras included Count Basie, Duke Ellington, Kay Kayser and Xavier Cugat.

Benny Goodman, Percy Faith, Morton Gould, Andre Kostelanetz, Paul Whiteman and many others wrote and arranged in the category of 'Symphonic Jazz.' In Symphonic Jazz, popular songs were arranged in a structured manner which employed the techniques of serious music forms. These songs were almost as structured as the repertory presented in formal concert halls.

1. Music from various sources of American styles competed for radio's _____ _____ which was the measuring rod, at that time, for the choice of the most popular songs.
2. These songs ranged from the 32-bar song or _____ type to Country-Western, serious Pop and Rhythm and Blues.

# DUKE ELLINGTON
## 1899-1975

Edward "Duke" Kennedy Ellington, the creator of the sophisticated Programmatic Jazz style, deserves special mention. Ellington was born in Washington, D.C., and

*Duke Ellington*

composed his first work when he was sixteen. Duke Ellington also had a talent for art and he was actually offered an art scholarship which he refused because he

wanted to be a musician, especially a pianist. Until the age of eighteen, Duke Ellington had no formal musical training, but he did teach himself to read music. He lived in Washington, D.C., where bands were in great demand.

There, Ellington joined two bands and eventually began booking bands himself. He soon organized a small group of five instrumentalists called the "Washingtonians" and later migrated to New York. With the Washingtonians, he began to create his own style of Jazz. In 1927, Duke Ellington became nationally recognized after opening in Harlem at the Cotton Club.

Duke Ellington wrote over 1000 tunes. Some of the best known are *I'm Beginning to See the Light, I Didn't Know About You, Don't You Know I Care?, In A Sentimental Mood, Mood Indigo, Sophisticated Lady, It's the Talk of the Town, Do Nothing 'Til You Hear From Me, Cottontail, Satin Doll* and *Solitude*. Ironically, Ellington's theme song *Take the A Train* was written by his collaborator, Billy Strayhorn.

Some of his programmatic symphonic type Jazz works include *Black, Brown and Beige,* a forty five minute musical fantasy portraying the history of the Black man in America; *Jump for Joy,* a musical comedy; and the film background scores for *Anatomy of a Murder* and *Paris Blues.* His musicals were never given a Broadway performance

The number of awards and honors received by Duke Ellington is numerous and includes citations from presidents and monarchs from Denmark, Sweden, France, Norway and England. Ellington also wrote sacred compositions including Jazz masses, sermons, cantatas, anthems, vocal solo works and music for television, films and radio. Duke Ellington's music firmly established him as one of the greatest American composers. He used an American-created art medium to express the ideas and feelings of his genius.

## RECALL

1. Duke Ellington composed his first composition when he was _____ years old.
2. Until the age of 18, Duke Ellington had no formal musical training but taught himself to _____ music.
3. In 1927 he became nationally recognized after opening in Harlem at the _____ Club.
4. Ellington wrote over _____ tunes.
5. He also wrote program _____ type jazz works.
6. "Jump for Joy" is one of his _____ comedies.
7. Ellington's music establishes him as one of America's greatest _____.

# JOHNNY MERCER
## 1909-1976

Johnny Mercer, a singer during the Swing Era, performed with Paul Whiteman and Benny Goodman. Mercer also wrote lyrics for many of the Hollywood movie musicals. *The Harvey Girls* featured the popular song, *On the Atchison, Topeka and the Santa Fe.* Mercer also wrote

the lyrics for the popular songs *Moon River* (1961) *The Days of Wine and Roses* (1962), *Blues in the Night* and *Autumn Leaves.* He also was one of the founders of Capitol Records.

## RECALL

1. Johnny Mercer performed with _____ _____ and Benny Goodman.
2. He wrote the lyrics for many of the Hollywood

movie _____.
3. Name two of his popular songs:
_____
_____

# Be-Bop, Cool and Funky Jazz
# 1940-1955

A revival of the New Orleans style Jazz (Dixieland) began around 1939 right in the middle of the Swing Era, and just before the advent of Be-Bop. This return to New Orleans Dixieland type jazz playing reached all the way to Europe, Japan, Australia, Uruguay, Holland and France.

The most imitated New Orleans artist was "King" Oliver. During this revival, White artists acknowledged the Black contributions which had been made. The Swing Era fostered the use of many Black Jazz arrangers and composers, as well as artists, by White conductors and directors. Nevertheless, many hotels on the road were unavailable to Black artists. The rental of certain concert or performance halls also depended on the racial identity of the performers. Radio stations promoted certain styles for different racial groups. Record companies recorded on separate labels for White and Black musicians.

The segregation problems contributed greatly to the emergence of Be-Bop. These problems developed a desire in young Black musicians to find a new path for the Jazz art forms. Young Black musicians sought to be different and did not want to simply return to an earlier style of Jazz or to be hemmed in by the popular use of Swing bands. Their experimentation was characterized by attempts at new sounds, polytonal conception (two or more tone centers), dissonance and tension, rapid tempos, strange modulations (key changes), exceptional technical difficulties and avoidance of singable melodies.

These ingredients were accompanied by a sort of 'hip' attitude which was to look down on any musician who was not able to perform Be-Bop. He was made to feel inferior. Musicians who tried to sit in were often shown what they could not do. Many times one soloist would interrupt another soloist near the end of his improvisation without the usual signal, such as the raising of a hand, to indicate some other soloist should begin playing. This would not have been done by the earlier jazz musicians and would have seemed almost disrespectful.

There were only a few masters of Be-Bop: Charlie "Bird" Parker (brain child of Be-Bop), Thelonius Monk (High Priest of Be-Bop), and John Birks "Dizzy" Gilliespie (1917-    ) who was years ahead of his time and was the foremost creator or father of Be-Bop. Having played in Cab Calloway's band, among others, Gilliespie was constantly experimenting with chords and sounds. He was a technical genius and developed agility equal to a virtuoso piano technique. Unusual for that time, he constantly seemed to be in search of his Afro-heritage which was reflected through his style of clothing. The musical revolution from 1940-1950, called Be-Bop, was led by Dizzy Gilliespie.

Thelonius Monk (1920-    ) was the third of the three major contributors to Be-Bop. The unusual harmonies and modulations which were some of the elements of Be-Bop were then called 'Zombie' music.

Monk was born in 1920 in Rocky Mount, North Carolina. He was one of the greatest Jazz composers. Monk also developed and was the leader of many small ensembles and combos. His keyboard improvisational ability was astounding. Among his outstanding compositions are *Criss-Cross* and *Well, You Needn't*.

Be-Bop was followed by another style of Jazz referred to as 'Cool Jazz'. Here the intricate difficulties of Bop were dismissed. The strain of using extreme ranges on instruments was eliminated. The tuba was used again. A sort of Baroque chamber music type Jazz feeling was evoked with the delicate, lyrical sound of the flute as a major solo instrument. There was more flexibility with the time signatures (meters). French horn, cello and oboe minus the over-exaggerated sounds or wide vibrato were featured on solos. The dynamics, attacks and releases were more structured and polished.

Cool Jazz was very much like classical music with many classical forms such as the rondo. One of the most influential of the Cool Jazz Era creators was Charlie Parker (1920-1955), nicknamed 'Yardbird' or 'Bird'. Parker's saxophone influenced many musicians and he was frequently imitated.

Parker had an unbelievable rhythmic feel and his lagging rhythm combined with his mastery of harmonic content and chordal structure. Parker's following of almost structured musical forms yet playing hot, but cool, made him the most copied of the Cool Jazz innovators.

The years betwen 1955 and 1960 saw a combination of all of the later Jazz forms. This was a fusion that included some of the Be-Bop harmonic elements. There was a free rhythmic flow often referred to as Funky—a happy-go-lucky type of enthusiastic rhythm, a relaxation of tension and use of the basic roots of many earlier Jazz styles. A title for this fusion of styles is hard to come by but a term such as Funky Jazz could well apply. Also applicable would be 'Hard' Jazz—a driving type of Jazz where Jazz piano players introduce a return to simple but fundamental Jazz playing.

Jazz development continues today in many categories from serious structured Jazz, like symphonic music to 'Soul' Jazz, to those who experiment with electronic contributions or avant-garde materials, styles, sounds and instruments. There will always be musicians who search for the new. Through them, Jazz will continue to live and grow as a great contribution America has made to the art of music.

## RECALL

1. A revival of the New Orleans style Jazz (Dixieland) began around _____.
2. The most imitated New Orleans artist was _____ _____.
3. The _____ Era promoted the use of many _____ jazz arrangers and composers.

4. John '_____ _____
   was the foremost creator or father of be-bop.
5. _____ _____ was
   called the High Priest of Be-Bop.
6. Be-bop was followed by another style of jazz
   referred to as _____.
7. Cool Jazz was very much like classical music
   with many classical forms such as the
   _____.
8. One of the most influential of the Cool Jazz Era
   creators was _____
   _____.
9. A title for this fusion of styles of jazz could be
   _____.

# Jazz Authors

## DAVID BAKER—BILLY TAYLOR
## QUINCY JONES

David Baker is an outstanding composer, conductor and writer of several books about Jazz.

Baker heads the Jazz Music Department at Indiana University. He has previously taught at two other colleges and also at the high school level. David Baker is considered an outstanding music educator and composer. His compositions are contemporary and innovative and he plays several instruments.

David Baker's Book, *Jazz Improvisation,* is used in schools and colleges all over the country

Billy Taylor is one of the talented and creative students of Undine Moore. He is a Jazz piano player as well as composer. His song, *I Wish I Knew How it Would Feel To Be Free*, is a favorite. Taylor has received an honorary degree from two universities and has made a name all over the world with his "Jazz Mobile" show. In addition, his movies have been very successul, and he has written over 11 books on Jazz. Taylor was once the musical director for the David Frost Show.

Quincy Jones, an outstanding trumpet player and pianist, has been a very prolific composer and contributor to contemporary American Jazz music. He studied with Nadia Boulanger and Villa-Lobos and at Seattle University as well as the Berkeley School of Music. Quincy Jones is one of the few writers of incidental and theme music for television using electronic and chance music.

He was born in Illinois and lives in California. Quincy Jones is the writer of the theme music for the television shows "Sanford and Sons," "The Bill Cosby Show" and "Roots" and also for the movies, "The Pawnbroker" and "In Cold Blood."

### RECALL

1. _____ is a composer, conductor and
   head of the Jazz Music Department at Indiana
   University.
2. Billy Taylor, the composer, has written 11 books
   on _____.
3. The outstanding composer who did the music
   for the television movie, *Roots*, is
   _____.

# MODERN AMERICA
## Classical
## From 1900

# MODERN AMERICA
## Classical
## From 1900
### The Twentieth Century
### The "ism" Period

The twentieth century is a period of "isms"—Individualism, Realism, Nationalism, Transitionalism, and Primitivism.

Both the old and new techniques, styles and forms are used. Musical combinations of Popular and Classical, Folk and Jazz, secular Blues (non-sacred) and sacred may be packaged for the concert stage. They may also be grouped for informal settings which require a less structured musical form. This informal style may be heard almost anywhere from an airport to a club. Composers reflect the ability to write using varied musical forms of expression. Often the musical forms are combined in a single composition, for example: Classical, Jazz, Folk, Gospel, electronic/computerized and even Rock.

These new Twentieth Century musical directions began about the end of the Impressionistic Period and reflect the following:

1. New rhythmic practices of combining two or more meters to be played simultaneously—called *Polymetrical*. (for example: 2/4 and 5/4)
2. New organizational concepts of tones which replace major and minor keys: regular key tonality with some dissonance, called *Pandiatoniscism;* two or more key centers at the same time, called *Polytonality;* and the absence of a tonal center, called *Atonality.*
3. A return to primitive cultures for additional musical ideas—expression through psychological introspection.
4. Use of noise: noise makers, forms of electronic music (synthesizers), tapes, computer music, or other complete changes of order as well as playing styles.
5. New systems of notating music.

## WILLIAM GRANT STILL
### 1895-

William Grant Still is called the 'Dean of America's Black Composers'. He was born May 11, 1895, in Woodville, Mississippi and went to the public schools in Little Rock, Arkansas. He went on to study at Wilberforce

University, Oberlin Conservatory on a scholarship, and the New England Conservatory.

Still studied privately with George W. Chadwick and Edgar Varese through scholarships made possible by them. He played in many orchestras and knew several instruments: the violin, the cello and the oboe. William Grant Still has orchestrated many works for outstanding musicians including W.C. Handy, Donald Voorhees, Sophie Tucker, Paul Whiteman, Willard Robison and Artie Shaw. He also arranged and conducted the Deep River Hour on CBS radio.

He conducted a number of his own works in 1936 when he was a guest conductor with the Los Angeles Philharmonic. Still was the first Black man to conduct any major symphony orchestra in the United States.

In 1955 he became the first of his race to conduct a major symphony in the South when he conducted the New Orleans Philharmonic Symphony Orchestra at Southern University.

Still has received many awards, among them the Guggenheim and Rosenwald Fellowships, an Honorary Degree of Master of Music from Wilberforce University in 1936, a Doctor of Music from Howard University in 1941, a Doctor of Music from Oberlin College in 1947 and a Doctor of Letters from Bates College in 1954.

He received the 1953 Freedom Foundation Award for his *To You America,* written to honor West Point's Sesquicentennial celebration. He has won other awards from the Columbia Broadcasting System, the New York World's Fair (1939-1940), Paul Whiteman, The League of Composers, the Cleveland Orchestra and the Southern Conference Educational Fund.

Mr. Still's works cover a wide musical area ranging from symphonies to operas.

1. William Grant Still is called the Dean of _____ _____ _____.

2. He was the first Black man to conduct a _____ _____ _____ in the United States.

3. His works range from _____ to _____.

# CHARLES GRIFFES
## 1884-1920

Charles Griffes was born in Elmira, New York. He was gifted in art and music. Griffes could do etchings, draw extremely well and paint with water colors.

As a high school student, Griffes decided to pursue a musical career and went to Germany to become a concert pianist. He studied with Rufer and the famous composer, Engelbert Humperdinck (1854-1921). After he began his study of theory with Humperdinck, he was so inspired by him that he was determined to become a composer.

Griffes returned to America in 1908 and in addition to composing, he taught music at the Hackley School in Tarrytown, New York. He wrote only a few works, but these works established him as an outstanding American composer.

There are three main periods of Griffes compositions: his early **student period** in which his music reflects the German School of his teachers Humperdinck and Rufer; the **second period** in which he makes use of some impressionistic techniques (French influence) and the **third period** where modern trends are reflected.

Griffes was an extremely hard worker and the excitement and extensive preparation for his orchestra tone poem, *Pleasure Dome of Kubla Khan,* proved too much for him and he died from overwork.

Griffes' works range from songs based on settings of German poems to piano pieces. His most exciting piano piece is *Roman Sketches* which is beautifully descriptive. It opens with *The White Peacock* which is presented with a leisurely chromatic theme; *Nightfall* which shows the various sounds of evening in a subdued calmness; and on to *The Fountain of 'Acqua Paola'* which pictures the rising and falling water with its glimmering, shimmering radiant effects; and then *Clouds* which begins with a majestic chordal passage suggesting a massive accumulation of clouds.

# JOHN ALDEN CARPENTER
## 1876-1951

John Alden Carpenter, a descendant of John Alden, was born in Park Ridge, Illinois, in 1876. He graduated from Harvard University and became a successful business man. During his leisure time Carpenter wrote music. Carpenter was a very dear friend of Carl Sandburg, the noted American poet-philosopher.

Carpenter's melodies are very American in rhythm and sound. His music is programmatic and nationalistic and paints a poetic picture of his ideas. One of his instrumental works, a suite in six movements, *Adventures in a Perambulator,* describes his adventurous morning rides in his baby carriage. Carpenter titles these adventures: *En Voiture* (in a carriage or perambulator), "The Policeman", "The Hurdy Gurdy" and "The Dogs". Carpenter also uses themes to identify himself, the Perambulator, the Nurse, the Policeman, Hurdy-Gurdy melodies and Dogs.

Carpenter was hailed by noted musicians and critics as a brilliant and significant writer of American music. His works include symphonies, ballets, songs, string quartets, quintets, suites, concertos and songs for children.

John Alden Carpenter

1. Charles Griffes studied with the famous composer, _____ _____

2. There are _____ main periods of Griffes' compositions.

3. His most exciting piano piece is "_____ _____."

4. _____ _____

_____ was a very dear friend of Carl Sandburg.

5. Carpenter's music is _____ and nationalistic.

6. "_____ _____ _____ _____" describes his adventurous morning rides in his baby carriage.

# CHARLES IVES
## 1874-1954

Charles Ives, America's first 'avante garde' (ahead of the guard'—meaning, ahead of the rest) composer, was born in Danbury, Connecticut. He received much of his musical inspiration from his musician father who was constantly seeking innovative means of musical expression. He was his son's first music teacher and taught Ives ear training making use of dissonance. It is reported that his father would have him sing a popular song (like *Swanee River)* in one key while he played the accompaniment in another key. This developed Ives' ability to hear the new sounds of polytonality.

Ives began his musical creativity with entirely free concepts. He experimented by using unusual instrumentation which would best express his ideas. In one of his works, Ives interrupts his piece to allow the instrumentalist to play whatever is wished because there is no written music.

Although Charles Ives was a recluse, his musical works reflect every aspect of American culture. His musical techniques were far ahead of his time. He made use of polyrhythms, strong dissonances, polyharmonies and atonality much earlier than other composers such as Stravinsky, Schoenberg, Berg and Webern, who are usually credited with these techniques.

Ives studied organ with Henry Shelley and attended Yale University where he studied with American composers Dudley Buck and Horatio Parker. During his college days he composed music and played the organ for a church. After obtaining his Bachelor of Arts degree, he worked as an insurance clerk in New York while serving as a part-time organist in a local church. He later opened his own insurance company and helped to found what today is known as Mutual of New York. Ives had no professional musical ambition and many of his works remained unknown, unpublished and unperformed for a long period of time.

His first publication issued privately, was *Sonata No. 2 for Piano* (1919 or 1920). It was written between 1909 and 1915. This sonata is actually a suite of four pieces with each piece having its own title: "Emerson", "Hawthorne", "The Alcotts" and "Thoreau". The music expresses the spirit of Transcendentalism (exploring beyond the basic techniques). This composition represents a programmatic, impressionistic picture of the four writers.

Ives received the Pulitzer Prize for Music in 1947 for his *Symphony No. 3*. He remained totally untouched by the recognition and impact of his music. There seems to be no music written by him after 1928. All of Ives' recognition for his musical works came late in his life.

# IGOR STRAVINSKY
## 1882-1974

*Igor Fredorovich Stravinsky*

The Twentieth century Russian composer and musical giant, Igor Stravinsky was born in Oranienbaum, a suburb of St. Petersburg, Russia. His father was an opera singer.

Stravinsky went to school and then on to college, hoping to please his father and become a lawyer. He had, however, an inner yearning for musical expression and soon found himself studying music theory books (harmony and counterpoint). He taught himself much of what he knew.

It was after that, the composer, Rimsky-Korsakoff taught Stravinsky the art of orchestration; Stravinsky was more interested in music than in law. Upon finishing his law course, he fell in love with a cousin whom he married. Through her he found much personal happiness because she was very understanding of his desire to become a musician. She encouraged him to leave the study of law and completely devote himself to music. This he did, and with the teaching and guidance of Rimsky-Korsakoff, began to write.

Stravinsky became one of the most controversial and prolific composers of the 20th century. He came to the United States on tour in 1925 and moved here after World War II. He became a United States citizen in 1945.

Stravinsky's works are numerous. However, three dances for the Paris Ballet Russe—*The Firebird* (L'oiseau de feu), *Petrouchka* and *The Rite of Spring* (Le sacre du printemps)—created the biggest stir during their performances.

Stravinsky has been established as a musical giant who broke away from the impressionistic and post-impressionistic musical styles.

## RECALL

1. _____ _____ was America's first avant-guarde composer.
2. Ives experimented by using _____ instrumentation which would best express his ideas.
3. Ives received the _____ _____ in music in 1947 for his "Symphony No. 3".
4. _____ _____ taught Stravinsky the art of orchestration.
5. Name two works Stravinsky wrote for the Ballet Russe: _____ and _____.

## WALTER PISTON
## 1894-1976

Walter Piston was born in Maine. He attended High School in Boston where he studied drawing and painting. During World War I he played in the Navy Band. After he left the Navy, he attended Harvard University.

He received the John Knowles Paine Scholarship and went to Paris where he remained for two years. In Paris he studied with Paul Dukas (1865-1935) and Nadia Boulanger. When he returned home he joined the faculty at Harvard.

Piston has received two Pulitzer Prizes for his *Third Symphony* and his *Seventh Symphony*. He has also received four honorary doctorates and numerous other awards.

Piston's music is difficult to classify. He writes according to the demands of the composition. Some of his works are difficult; some are simple. His balance and form are well laid out and constructed. He is easily identified as a modern composer. His modern techniques are present although they do not stand out boldly. They seem very native or second nature to Piston.

### RECALL

1. Walter Piston played in the _____ _____ during World War I.
2. He studied with Paul _____ and Nadia Boulanger.
3. He received _____ Pulitzer Prizes.
4. Piston writes according to the _____ of the composition.

## PAUL HINDEMITH
## 1895-1963

Paul Hindemith has become the most important composer of the early 1900's. He combined the 1700's traditional techniques with contemporary techniques and theory and began the neo-classical style of writing.

Hindemith was born in Hanau, Germany. As a youngster, the violin was his instrument and he entertained in many cafe-theatres and dance halls. He attended the Conservatory in his city and became an outstanding violinist. After marrying the daughter of the conductor of the Frankfurt Opera Company, he went to live in Berlin. There he became Professor of Composition for the Berlin High School for Music. Hindemith remained in Berlin until Hitler came to power. He was disliked by the Nazis because his wife was half Jewish and he frequently gave concerts with other Jewish musicians. They considered Hindemith's music controversial. He was finally forced to leave Germany and his music was banned from all programs there. Hindemith was invited to Turkey and eventually immigrated to America in 1940 and taught at Yale University. Hindemith became an American citizen in 1946.

His ideas on theory have been included in most important college and university music courses and his book, *The Craft of Musical Composition* is considered the most valuable contribution to music composition since the treatise of Rameau.

Ironically, Hindemith conducted his last public concert in the country that had banned his music—Berlin on November 12, 1963. The occasion was the premiere performance of a mass written by him for a cappella choir. He died on December 28 of the same year.

Paul Hindemith

### RECALL

1. Paul _____ has become the most important composer of the early 1900's.
2. He began the _____ - _____ style of writing.
3. His ideas on _____ have been included in most important college and university courses.

## ULYSSES SIMPSON KAY
## 1917-

Ulysses Kay was born in Tucson, Arizona, and was graduated from the University of Arizona in 1938. He attended the Eastman School of Music in Rochester where he received an M.A. degree in composition. Kay had the opportunity through scholarships to study with Paul Hindemith at Yale University. While in college he was encouraged by the Dean of American Black Composers, William Grant Still.

Kay came from a musical family. His brother played the violin; his mother and sister, the piano. His maternal uncle was the famous jazz genius, "King" Oliver.

While playing with the Navy Band during World War II, he had the opportunity of learning to play many instruments and compose and arrange for them. At the end of the war, Kay continued to study composition at Columbia University after receiving the Ditson Fellowship. He also received a Fulbright Scholarship, the Prix de Rome, the Guggenheim Fellowship and an

honorary doctoral degree from Bucknell University and Lincoln University in Pennsylvania, Illinois Wesleyan University and the University of Arizona.

Kay was selected as one of the American composers to be sent to Russia on a cultural exchange mission sponsored by the State Department and he has taught at Lehman College City University in New York.

His works range from symphonies and operas, to suites, quartets and concertos. His most popular works include *The Quiet One* (the movie score music), *The Serenade for Orchestra, Three Pieces After Blake* and his two operas, *The Boor* and *The Juggler of Our Lady*. Kay's music reflects the Neo-Classical influence.

### RECALL

1. Ulysses Kay studied with Paul
   _____.

2. He was selected as one of the American composers to be sent to _____.

3. His most popular works include the movie score for "_____ _____
   _____".

## HOWARD HANSON
## 1896-

Howard Hanson, born in Wahoo, Nebraska, studied at Luther College, the New York Institute of Musical Art and Northwestern University. He taught theory and composition at the College of the Pacific in San Jose, California, and became Dean of the school's Conservatory of Fine Arts.

Hanson was able to travel to Rome after winning the Prix de Rome of the American Academy. While he was in Rome, he began composing. Among his early works was his first symphony, *Nordic*. This symphony was performed in Rome in 1923. He returned to America where he was appointed to the position of Director of the Eastman School of Music in Rochester, New York.

Hanson is regarded as one of the pioneers of the Neo-Romantic School of Music. (Neo-Romantic is defined as music of contemporary style, technique and language with the stress on emotional content.) Hanson composed several symphonic poems, many concertos, an opera, *Merry Mount* and various other works. His most noted work, his symphony called *Romantic*, truly represents Hanson's inner emotional feelings and love of lyrical expression. Hanson has stated that he feels contemporary music shows signs of becoming too intellectual.

Howard
Harold
Hanson

### RECALL

1. Howard Hanson studied at Luther College, New York Institute of Musical Art and
   _____ University.

2. He was appointed to the position of Director of the _____ School of Music.

# ROY HARRIS
## 1898-

Roy Harris was born in Lincoln County, Oklahoma. He studied philosophy and economics at the University of California (at Los Angeles) and made time to study harmony. He continued his music studies privately with Arthur Farwell.

Harris has held various musical positions at Westminister Choir College in Princeton, New Jersey, Cornell University, the National Institute of Music in Puerto Rico and at the University of California at Los Angeles.

Harris has a style that is so truly his own that it is easily recognizable. His music has pure American quality. He uses the techniques of the twentieth century with taste and moderation. His harmonic use of dissonance with rhythmic variation combine to make his music personal and attractive yet contemporary and sophisticated.

His *Symphony No. 4* (Folk Song Symphony), scored for chorus and orchestra, incorporates the American folk songs *When Johnny Comes Marching Home, Oh Bury Me Not on the Lone Prairie, Jump Up My Lady, The Blackbird* and *The Crow.* They are all cleverly interwoven throughout the various movements. This is a functional work which can be used by schools and colleges.

Harris has composed more than seven symphonies and numerous other works. His best known orchestral works are his *Symphony No. 3* and the American overture, *When Johnny Comes Marching Home.*

## RECALL

1. Roy Harris' music has a _____ American quality.
2. His _____ use of dissonance with rhythmic variation combine to make his music personal.
3. Harris' best known orchestral work is his "_____ _____ _____".

# EDGAR VARESE
## 1883-1965

Edgar Varese was born in Paris. He had every intention of becoming an engineer. It was the preparation for this field which gave him his solid background in science and mathematics. He did, however, change his mind and pursued a career of music. He went to several different music schools, among them Paris Conservatoire. After Paris, he went on to Germany where he actually conducted and composed. He came to the United States in 1915 and settled in New York where he did much to promote new music.

Varese is a master of new, inventive sounds in contemporary music. He has made use of all possible methods of imitating and making noises to create sounds for his compositions. He describes his own music as organized sound.

Varese's early music was exciting and it created interest all over our country. About 1934 his attention turned to the study of science and mathematics and the theoretical side of music. His lost interest in composition was not restored until about 1955 when he devoted himself to electronic music.

His *Hyperprism* for winds and percussion created a stir and an album of his major works was issued by Columbia Records in 1960. Varese died in 1965.

# JOHN CAGE
## 1912-

John Cage was born in Los Angeles, California on September 5, 1912. He studied with Varese, Schoenberg, Weiss, Cowell and with Lazare Levy in Paris. Cage's early influence was the twelve-tone system, but he soon abandoned it in search of something new. He expressed a particular interest in the percussive instruments and rhythms.

Cage felt the need for composers to find a completely new creative means of expressing musical ideas with new sounds and old and new instruments. He experimented with:

*Chance music* (aleatory music)—music which is created by each performer as they go along.
*Concrete music*—music reproduced on tape frequently using alteration and distortion of sounds previously recorded.
*Neo-Dadaism*—the use of nonsense devices as a mock expression of escape from life's disappointing realities.

Cage invented the prepared piano (a method of re-tuning a piano in order to create unusual percussive effects). He also experimented with sounds from different sources (anything that created noise): tin cans, rattles, paper, running water, etc.

Cage received many awards, among them the Guggenheim Fellowship. His *Foutana Mix,* written in 1958 for magnetic tape, is the best known of his works.

## RECALL

1. Edgar Varese had every intention of becoming an _____ and studied science and mathematics.
2. He is a master of new, inventive _____ in contemporary music.
3. His lost interest in composition was restored in 1955 when he devoted himself to _____ music.
4. John Cage's early influence was the _____ _____ system.
5. He invented the _____ piano.
6. He also experimented with sounds from different sources — anything that created _____.

## KATHLEEN K. DAVIS
### 1892-1941

Kathleen K. Davis was a noted composer, teacher and author. She studied with Nadia Boulanger and Stuart Mason. Among her works are the symphonic poem. *The Burial of a Queen,* a cantata, *This is Noel* and numerous choral works for various choir groupings which are sung all over the world. Katherine K. Davis' works are Neo-Classical in style and show a great gift of melody. Her understanding of the voice adds a particular excitement to her choral works.

## UNDINE SMITH MOORE
### 1904-

Undine Smith Moore, composer, teacher, lecturer and arranger, was born in Jarrat, Virginia, and is a graduate of Fisk University. She also attended Columbia, Eastman and Julliard Schools of Music and now teaches music theory at Virginia Union University.

Among her works are the *Afro-American Suite for Cello and Piano, Three pieces for Flute and Piano, Hail, Warrior* and numerous arrangements of Spirituals and other works. She shows great understanding of form and structure. Her music displays *Pandiatonicism* (traditional harmonies with dissonance added).

## RECALL

1. Kathleen K. Davis studied with _____ _____.
2. Her works are _____ in style.
3. Undine Smith Moore's music displays _____.

# KURT WEILL
## 1900-1950

Kurt Weill (German-American composer) developed a combination of musical comedy and opera in Germany called the Song Play. The Song Play included popular tunes, jazz, ballads, arias, cannons, classic music, romantic music and dance tunes. There is always a libretto or story usually based on current trends and events.

Kurt Weill wanted to reach the masses of people through his Song Plays. Some of his Song Plays are *Der Protagonist* (written especially for school) with a text by Georg Kaiser; *Die Dreigroschenoper* (usually referred to as the *Three Penny Opera)* which is one of his most classic and popular Song Plays; and *Down In The Valley;* a folk opera in one act. This opera incorporated five folk songs from the Kentucky mountain region: *Down in the Valley, Sourwood Mountain, The Lonesome Dove, The Little Black Train* and *Hop Up, My Ladies.*

When Hitler came to power, the Weills left Germany and, in 1935, came to the United States. Kurt Weill became an American citizen in 1943. While in America he became a very popular Broadway show composer with *Johnny Johnson—(a satirical Song Play against war) which appeared on Broadway in* 1936; *Knickerbocker Holiday—* 1938; *Lady In The Dark—1941; One Touch of Venus—* 1943; *Street Scene—*1947; and *Lost in the Stars—*1949.

## RECALL

1. Kurt Weill developed a combination of musical comedy and opera in Germany called

   _____ _____.

2. "_____

   _____" is one of his most classic and popular song plays.

3. The "Song Play" has a story based on

   _____.

# AARON COPLAND
## 1900-

Aaron Copland is a composer, author, writer, conductor and pianist. He has traveled all over the world giving piano concerts and guest conducting.

Copland was born in Brooklyn, New York, on November 14, 1900, where his studies on the piano began at the age of 14. He later went to France where he studied at a school of music and was afforded the rare privilege of studying privately with the master theory teacher, Nadia Boulanger (1887-    ). It was Miss Boulanger who introduced a work Copland wrote for her, *Symphony for Organ and Orchestra,* to the American public in 1925.

Copland was able to secure adequate financial assistance and fellowships to enable him to devote full time to composition.

Copland worked diligently to promote the contemporary works of American composers. He is, along with Roger Sessions (1896-    ), the organizer of the Copland-Sessions Concerts for Young American Composers and the founder of the American Festival of Contemporary Music. He also supports various groups who contribute financially to contemporary American composers.

He has authored several books: *What To Listen For in Music, Our New Music, Copland On Music* and *Music and Imagination.*

Copland's music reflects his ability to write in many styles. Some of his music shows Romantic influences while other of his works show a great deal of dissonance and abstractness. In many of his early compositions, Copland made use of jazz music. His works range from piano pieces, to theater music, to sonatas, symphonies and ballets to film scores. *Billy the Kid, Rodeo* and *Appalachian Spring* are three very popular ballets.

Aaron Copland received the first Guggenheim Fellowship awarded a composer in 1925 and later was awarded the Edward MacDowell Medal. In 1946 he became the Dean of the Berkshire Music Center at Tanglewood.

Aaron
Copland

## RECALL

1. Aaron Copland is a _____,

   _____, _____

   and pianist.

2. He studied in France with the master theory teacher _____ _____.

3. Copland worked diligently to promote the contemporary works of _____

   _____.

4. Copland's music reflects his ability to write in many _____.

5. He received the first _____

   _____ awarded a composer.

6. Name two of Aaron Copland's ballets:

   _____ and _____.

# SAMUEL BARBER
## 1910-

Samuel Barber, an outstanding American composer, was born in Westchester, Pennsylvania. He had a job as an organist before he was twelve. His Aunt was a famous singer.

The influence of Barber's exposure to his famous aunt's contralto singing is heard in the lyrical elements of his compositions. His melodies have soaring qualities.

Barber attended the Curtis Institute of Music in Philadelphia. There he studied composition, piano and voice. He won the Pulitzer Scholarship and also the American Prix de Rome Award, among others.

It was Arturo Toscanini (1867-1957), then conductor of the N.B.C. Symphony Orchestra, who introduced two of Barber's works, *Adagio for Strings* and *Essay for Orchestra,* to the American public. Barber's works range from songs to works for orchestra to piano chamber music to operas.

In 1966 The Metropolitan Opera Company relocated in its new theater at the Lincoln Center for the Performing Arts in New York. On September 16, Samuel Barber's opera, *Antony and Cleopatra* (based on a Shakespearean drama), written especially for this gala opening, was premiered before a dazzling and important audience. Leontyne Price was Cleopatra, Justino Diaz was Antony and Thomas Schippers conducted. Franco Zeffrelli, the writer of the libretto, was also responsible for the staging and costuming.

## RECALL

1. Samuel Barber was exposed to his famous aunt's _____ _____ which influenced the lyrical elements of his compositions.

2. _____ _____ introduced two of Barber's works to the American public.

3. Samuel Barber's opera "Antony and Cleopatra" was written especially for the gala opening of the _____ _____ for the _____ _____ in New York.

# GIAN CARLO MENOTTI
## 1911-

Gian Carlo Menotti is known as the composer who has helped renew interest in opera.

Menotti was born in Italy and, like Mozart, he was a child prodigy and started composing when very young. He wrote his first opera when he was eleven.

Menotti came to America in 1928. He attended the Curtis Institute and studied with Rosario Scalero. Menotti's opera, *Amelia Goes to the Ball* (Amelia al Ballo), was written when he was only twenty-three. He also wrote the libretto. Since this opera was a success, he went on to write *The Old Maid and the Thief,* again writing the libretto himself. Among his other operas, for which he also wrote the librettos, are *The Telephone* (comic opera), *The Consul, Labyrinth, The Last Savage, The Medium, The Saint of Bleecker Street* and *Martin's Lie.* In addition, he wrote *The Death of the Bishop of Brandisi* (a cantata), *The Unicorn, the Gorgon and the Manicore* (a madrigal ballet) and his most famous and frequently performed work, *Amahl and the Night Visitors,* for which he again wrote the libretto.

Menotti possesses a clear understanding of theatre. His scores lend themselves toward the comic view. His music fully establishes the moods called for in his works. Menotti also seems to use whatever musical school he needs to express his ideas in a neo-classical manner.

Menotti received several grants, scholarships and awards. He wrote the libretto for the opera, *Vanessa,* composed by his good friend, Samuel Barber.

## RECALL

1. _____ _____ _____ is known as the composer who has helped renew interest in opera.

2. His most famous and frequently performed work is "_____ _____ _____ _____ ."

3. Menotti also seems to use whatever musical school he needs to express himself in a _____ manner.

## NORMAN DELLO JOIO
## 1913-

Norman Dello Joio, a student of Paul Hindemith, was born in New York and began his early studies with his father, a church organist. His later studies were at Julliard and the Berkshire Music Center and Tanglewood.

Dello Joio uses the musical forms of earlier periods but adds new modern rhythmic patterns and harmonies. His music is lyrical and often reflects the free style of the early Gregorian chants. The Catholic Church liturgical music seems to have influenced him.

Dello Joio has won numerous awards, among them the Pulitzer Prize in 1957 for his *Meditations on Ecclesiastics* and the New York Critics Award for his orchestral work *Variations, Chaconne and Finale.*

He has taught at Sarah Lawrence College in New York and Mannes College of Music. His life was reviewed on CBS television on a program called "Profile of a Composer" in 1958.

## RECALL

1. Norman Dello Joio was a student of _____ _____

2. His music is lyrical and often reflects the free style of the early _____ chants.

3. He received the New York Critics Award for his orchestral work "_____ _____ _____ ."

## LEONARD BERNSTEIN
## 1918-

Leonard Bernstein is a conductor, composer, pianist, lecturer and artist. He was born in Lawrence, Massachusetts, and has studied at Harvard with another noted

composer, Walter Piston. He further studied conducting with Fritz Reiner while attending the Curtis Institute in Philadelphia and studied compositon with another great composer, Randall Thompson.

In response to his obvious musical awareness, he received scholarships to the Tanglewood Music Center where he had the opportunity to study with Serge Koussevitzky. Bernstein soon became an assistant teacher at Tanglewood and established himself as a conductor in November of 1943 when he replaced Bruno Walter who was to conduct the New York Philharmonic Orchestra. His reputation as a conductor grew and he has conducted concerts all over the world. From 1958 until his resignation in 1969, he was musical director of the New York Philharmonic Orchestra. Since his resignation he has devoted himself to composition.

Bernstein's works include many Broadway musicals and stage productions, among them the musical comedy *On the Town* and the famous musical *West Side Story.* He has written music for movies and he often lectures on television using an orchestra to demonstrate. His two books, *The Joy of Music* and *The Infinite Variety of Music* are a combination of his lecture scripts from television. Bernstein's works range from symphonies to ballets, works for choir and soloists and overtures. His Symphony No. 1, called *Jeremiah Symphony,* Symphony No. 2 for piano and orchestra entitled *The Age of Anxiety,* and his *Overture to Candide* for orchestra are just three of this prolific composer-conductor's compositions.

1. Leonard Bernstein studied conducting with Fritz _____.
2. He became an assistant teacher at _____.
3. From 1958 to 1969 Leonard Bernstein was conductor of the _____ _____ Philharmonic Orchestra.
4. What was Bernstein's most famous musical comedy? _____

## GEORGE THEOPHILUS WALKER
### 1927-

George Walker was born in Washington, D.C. He attended Oberlin College, the Curtis Institute, studied in France and the Eastman School of Music. Among others, he studied with Nadia Boulanger, Gian Carlo Menotti and Rudolf Serkin. Walker assisted Serkin at the Curtis Institute and taught at the Dalcroze School of Music in New York, Smith College, Dillard University in New Orleans and at Rutgers University.

Walker is a noted composer and concert pianist. His concert tours have taken him through America, Europe and the East Indies. He has written music for orchestra, piano, and voice that is contemporary in style and technique.

His music is difficult and demands excellent technical skills. He uses both tonal and atonal sounds and expressions with very complex and exciting rhythms. His *Piano Sonata No. 1* is based on a Kentucky folksong *Oh Bury Me Beneath the Willow* and a folksong taken from Carl Sandburg's *Songbag*. His sonata is recorded on Desto Records with pianist Natlie Hinderas.

Walker has received numerous awards, among them being the Harvey Gaul Prize for his *Sonata for Two Pianos* in 1964.

1. George Walker studied with Nadia _____, Menotti and Rudolf Serkin.
2. His music is difficult and demands excellent _____ skills.
3. His "_____ _____ No. 1" is based on a Kentucky folksong and a folksong from Carl Sandburg's "Songbag".

## LOUIS W. BALLARD

Louis W. Ballard is a noted American composer. He is a descendant of both the Sioux and the Cherokee Americans. Ballard studied at the University of Tulsa and the University of Oklahoma.

His compositions include works for orchestra, ballet, chorus and arrangements of collections of his native folk music.

Louis W. Ballard has received various awards and grants including the first Marion Nevins MacDowell Award. He received this award for his woodwind quintet, *Ritmo Indio*. He has recorded authentic Early American songs on Canyon Records and is currently a specialist for the music curriculum department of the United States Department of the Interior's Bureau of Indian Affairs.

His published cantata *The Gods Will Hear* for soloist, mixed chorus, piano and percussion is one of this most popular works.

## RECALL

1. Louis W. Ballard is a descendant of both the _____ and the _____ Americans.
2. He studied at the University of Tulsa and the University of _____.
3. His published cantata "_____ _____ _____" is one of his most popular works.

# MODERN AMERICA

# Country, Folk, Blues and Gospel From 1900

# MODERN AMERICA
## Country, Folk, Blues and Gospel
## From 1900

The music now called Country-Western may be traced back to the new arrivals in the Appalachian areas. Country-Western today may be divided into two forms and two styles:

1. Country and Western — Ozark and Appalachian Mountains.
2. Bluegrass and Cowboy — Southwest and Plains.

## Country and Western

Country-Western music highly reflects its regional surroundings and the traditional occupations of its peoples. The early physical and geographical isolation of the Appalachian arrivals from the rest of the Eastern and Midwestern communities led them into perpetuating, developing and expressing mostly their own culture and styles. The Appalachian highlands were particularly isolated.

Many English people settled in the highlands about the end of the eighteenth century. The English ballad-type songs which they brought with them have been traditionally passed on to each new generation. Northern and Southern Appalachian versions of some of the songs developed, but most of them were very similar to one another. The text of an English folksong usually spoke of castles, ladies, knights and ships and represented the earlier age of chivalry.

*Billy Boy, Sourwood Mountain, Barbara Allen, and The Hangman's Song* are songs which can be directly traced to early English folklore.

The occupations of the people of the Appalachian Mountain area were largely centered around the jobs necessary for ordinary existence in an agricultural economy — raising their own crops and sheep and cattle, making their own clothes, building their own homes and churches and providing their own entertainment.

Early Appalachian settlers often bartered or exchanged merchandise or products without using money. The system and services of a modern industrial society remained remote. The law was administered by the individual. This gave rise to feuding families like the Hatfield's and the McCoy's who took the law into their own hands. Some of these family feuds continued for years.

The Appalachian peoples created their own versions of the English ballad. The songs were of a rather easy narrative form and told a complete story. They used simple chord progressions and uncomplicated melodies that were emotionally touching. The texts were based on everyday life experiences of love, death, fear, work, play, and sometimes, even nonsense.

Nashville and Memphis became the Country-Western music capitols. Country-Western records and shows have been produced and sold to an over-expanding percentage of the American public. The Grand Ole Opry became the Hit Parade of Country-Western music during the radio era and continued down into the era of television.

Some famous folk performers and Country-Western artist-composers are Red Foley, Chet Atkins, Hank Thompson, Hank Williams (1923-1953), Eddie Arnold, Earl Scruggs, Lester Flatt, Johnny Cash, Charlie Pride and Glen Campbell. There are also many female Country-Western artist-composers such as Tami Wynett, Bobbi Gentry and Dolly Parsons.

Ryman Auditorium in downtown Nashville was the home of these famous W.S.M. Radio Country concert stars. These concerts were held every Friday and Saturday nights for 33 seasons.

Most of today's Country-Western artists represent the new faces and social customs of the area from which this American music comes. Three of the very early, traditional Country-Western songs are still popular all over the world—*Ground Hog, Red River Valley* and *Down in the Valley.* You will remember that Kurt Weill, the German-American composer, wrote an operetta in which *Down in the Valley* is the main melody throughout.

In 1974, the Grand Ole Opry moved to a new 4,400 seating capacity, air conditioned building. This building is away from downtown Nashville at Briley Parkway, north of Lebanon Road and south of Gallatin Road. This entire new area of 110 acres is a park of shows, zoos, rides, restaurants and gift shops.

Radio and television brought urban styles and awareness to much of Appalachia, and Country Western music absorbed much commercial influence. Country-Western now includes not only folk, but also Blues, Jazz and Popular characteristics.

## Bluegrass and Cowboy

As the earlier workers of the Southwest and Plains drove their cattle and worked, they sang. These songs, which talked about the outdoors, the working conditions and their personal feelings are called 'Cowboy' songs. Most of the Cowboy songs have folk music characteristics or are composed in a folk music style.

The categories of Cowboy songs range from lullabies to ballads of outlaws and 'dogie' songs. Lullabies were sung to keep the animals still at night. Ballad songs were sung to express the cowboy's feelings or tell a story of some known person, and dogie songs were used to stop stampedes.

Of the popular cowboy music artists, Roy Rogers and Gene Autry were among the first to be seen in the movies and heard on records throughout America. They influenced the record industry which promoted cowboy music that had been used in movies and on television.

# Folk Songs

There are many ballad folk singers who have sung traditional folk songs in the traditional manner with an attempt to preserve all of the pure characteristics of the music: voice inflection, twang, slides, cries, delivery, style and performance with proper accompaniment and instruments. All are part of a true folk music performance artistry. Folk singers who collect, perform and preserve the folk music heritage in its original historical form with little if any, changes are: Burl Ives, Pete Seeger, Josh White, Leon Bibb and Alan Lomax.

Most early folk music was unaccompanied. And when accompaniments were used, the instruments were the fiddle (violin), guitar, banjo, mandolin, accordian, dulcimer and piano.

### RECALL

1. The music now called Country-Western music may be traced back to the new arrivals in the _____ areas.

2. Country-Western music highly reflects its regional surroundings and the _____ occupations of its peoples.

3. The Appalachian peoples created their own versions of the _____ ballad.

4. _____ were sung to keep the animals still at night.

5. _____ _____ collect, perform and preserve the folk music heritage in its original form.

6. Most early folk music was _____.

7. The work song usually required a _____ _____

Burl Ives

# Workgang Songs

Workgang songs were generally sung while the men worked to ease their workload and to keep the group working at a required pace. Hammering, rowing or hauling to songs made the work day pass faster.

The work song usually required a song leader. He had to select the appropriate songs, inspire the men into a willingness to sing (and work), and keep the songs flowing in a manner which would not interrupt the continuity of the work.

The workgang songs have been found to be very important to the total day's productivity. Songleaders in workgangs who made poor selections of songs were immediately replaced.

For the workers (who were usually slaves or prisoners) these songs represented an outlet for expressing their personal feelings about their social status and predicament.

# The Blues

It was shortly after the Emancipation Proclamation in 1863, when Black men and women were suddenly freed from slavery without adequate jobs, money or places to live. Most of the men were forced to become migratory workers, providing, of course, that there was work available.

They sang about their troubles, their social conditions and their personal problems. As migratory workers, many were separated from their families. Singing on street corners, in bars and at dances and parties for any money they could collect became a way of life. Railroad stations always provided ready audiences while travelers were waiting for trains.

These men soon became known as traveling Musical Bards. Some of them even put their music down on paper and sold it after their performances in order to get money. The women who had to remain home also expressed their loneliness, despair and suffering through the singing of the "Blues".

These early Blues were folk or country Blues. The language was bold and vivid. They told the performer's true story with no feelings spared.

## W. C. HANDY
## 1873-1958

William Christopher (W.C.) Handy, born in Florence, Alabama, became known as the 'Father of the Blues'. Performing along with him on a program one night was a group of country artists playing a new type of music. The group had upset the audience with a new sound. The new music of Blues was then thought to be not at all respectable. It was considered to belong to the untrained Black musicians and traveling bards.

But, W.C. Handy was so impressed and influenced by the Blues that he, although a trained musician, immediately began to write using the 'blues' form. Among his works are *The Memphis Blues* (written in 1909 and published in 1912, *The Beale Street Blues* (a campaign song for mayoral candidate Edward H. Crump from Tennessee), *The Yellow Dog Blues, St. Louis Blues* (published in 1914—now a classic), *Joe Turner Blues, Careless Blues, Hesitating Blues, Harlem Blues, John Henry Blues, Friendless Blues* and *Basement Blues*.

Handy's other compositions include over sixty works: anthems, arranged marches, work songs and symphonic works. He also exposed the Blues to the American concert halls and dance enthusiasts. Because of his fame from his *Memphis Blues*, W.C. Handy was able to establish a professional musical organization which could book over fifty men nightly to play dance jobs in Tennessee and surrounding states. This exposure greatly matured and spread the instrumental style of blues which would later in turn give birth to Jazz.

Since the blues written by W.C. Handy were notated and scored, they were accessible to all of the music community, the White as well as the Black.

W.C. Handy also established the Blues in the American musical scene through three major contributions. To the three-line form Blues verse he added a *fourth line verse* (as the second part of the *St. Louis Blues*). Then Handy laid the groundwork for the eventual *thirty-two bar* popular American song style (adopted by commercial pop writers in New York's Tin-Pan Alley) which became the basis for America's Pop song industry. Finally, he used Latin American dance forms such as the habanera in *Memphis Blues* and the tango in *St. Louis Blues*.

W.C. Handy also wrote his autobiography, *Father of the Blues*, a book of Black spirituals, articles and informative literature, and a book on Black music and musicians. He was also the owner of a publishing company (W.C. Handy), a schoolteacher, organized his own band and even worked in the iron mills.

W.C. Handy

Handy was an excellent cornet player and toured extensively with his band before losing his eyesight. Because of his outstanding musicianship, the city of Memphis dedicated a park to him where a statue of Handy holding his beloved cornet now stands.

A second early blues contributor was Gertrude Pridgett, known as "Ma" Rainey. She is called the 'Mother of the Blues'. "Ma" Rainey first heard blues around 1902 while touring with a musical show troupe called the Rabbit Foot Minstrel Company. An unidentified young lady from a small Missouri town sang in an interesting and unusual new musical style. "Ma" Rainey was so impressed with this style that she asked the young lady to teach it to her. "Ma" then included one of the songs she learned in her minstrel show act as an encore. However, it received such an ovation that it later won a select place in her program.

"Ma" Rainey traveled throughout the South singing the Blues in theatres, meeting houses, taverns and cabarets. She became famous as one of the great Blues singers. She was also probably the first professional female Blues singer. "Ma" Rainey claimed that she gave these new style songs the name 'Blues'. She was constantly asked what kind of music this was. According to an interview by John W. Work, Jr., who was a noted Black composer (1901-1967), "Ma" Rainey replied to this question, "It's the Blues!"

In fairness to other Blues singer, however, there is some question about "Ma" Rainey's claim of originating the term 'Blues.' She said that fire destroyed newspaper clippings which mentioned her singing these then new songs as early as 1905. She maintained that after she began singing Blues songs, she often heard these same songs in the various towns and cities through which she had traveled. "Ma" Rainey was the bridge between the early less-structured country or Rural Blues Style and the era of the structured Classic Blues Style (1920).

"Ma" Rainey influenced many future Blues singers, including Bessie Smith (1894-1937) who was "Ma" Rainey's foremost student. Bessie Smith had also been a member of the Rabbit Foot Minstrel Company. "Ma" Rainey made her first recording in 1923 and continued to record for Paramount Records 12000 series for seven years.

"Ma" Rainey was often accompanied by Georgia Tom and his band. Georgia Tom was later to become known as Thomas A. Dorsey (1899-    ), 'The Father of Black Gospel Music'.

## RECALL

1. W.C. Handy became known as the
   _____ _____
   _____ _____.

2. The new music or _____ was then thought of as being not at all respectful.

3. Handy exposed the Blues to the American _____ _____ and dance enthusiasts.

4. He laid the groundwork for the eventual _____ _____ popular American song style.

5. Name two of his most popular Blues:
   _____ and _____.

6. _____ _____ is called the 'Mother of the Blues'.

7. She was also probably the _____ professional female Blues singer.

8. Ma Rainey was the bridge between the early _____ - _____ country or Rural Blues Style and the era of the _____ _____ Blues.

9. _____ _____ was Ma Rainey's foremost student.

# The Classical Blues Era
# 1920-1929

From about 1920 through 1929, blues music was made available to the public, especially Black communities, by commercial record companies. Since most men were migratory workers, the singers were usually women. Accompaniments were on the piano only because there were few jazz instrumentalists.

The first 'Classic Blues' recording was made by Mamie Smith in the early '20's and was called *Crazy Blues*. It was written by Perry Bradford (1893-    ), a Black composer. Okeh Recording Company recorded and distributed it. It broke all sales records of the time by selling 7,500 records in one week. *Crazy Blues* established the tremendous potential for selling blues records to the Black community. It also established the term 'Race Records' — records made especiailly for the Black community by talented singers from their community. And it began special labels or numbers for these recording companies. (Example: Decca Series 7000-8000 and Columbia Series 6000.) Other active companies in Blues production included Victor, Bluebird and Paramount. *Crazy Blues* encouraged

recording companies to hire Black talent scouts in order to secure the best Black talent both vocally and instrumentally.

Mamie Smith's recording opportunity came by chance. Sophie Tucker, a nationally famous White Pop singer, had first been signed by Okeh Recording Company to record *Crazy Blues*. She became ill and Mamie Smith was booked to replace her.

"Ma" Rainey's first recording was made in 1923. She used an instrumental combo for accompaniment (Louis Armstrong was on trumpet). Bessie Smith (1894-1937), the student protege of "Ma" Rainey, was called the 'Empress the Blues'. Fletcher Henderson (1898-1952) and Louis Armstrong were among those instrumentalists who accompanied her. Bessie Smith was a great vocalist who had a great voice and a definite influence on Blues singer Billie Holiday.

Although the Classic Blues Era was dominated by female singers, there were also some great male Blues singers. Blind "Lemon" Jefferson (1897-1929) traveled and sang for parties and dances for 15 years. In 1925, Paramount Records began recording him. "Lemon" made over eighty records for Paramount. His Blues songs provided a vivid picture of the life of Black people during this period. He composed many of his songs. Although some other male blues singers had been recorded earlier, Blind "Lemon" Jefferson's style, voice quality and masterful guitar playing had a great influence on the Blues singers who followed him. Among them was "Muddy Waters" (McKinley Morganfield) who was discovered in Stovall, Mississippi about 1942 and is one of the greatest Blues singers.

Other male Blues singers were "Leadbelly" Ledbetter (1888-1949), "Big Bill" Broonzy (1893-1958) and Lonnie Johnson (1889-    ). They made over 700 records sometimes using Duke Ellington or Louis Armstrong to accompany them.

Leadbelly

Bessie Smith

## RECALL

1. Between 1920 and 1929 'Blues' music was made available to the public (especially Black communities) by commercial _____ companies.

2. The first Classic Blues recording was made by Mamie Smith and was called "_____ _____".

3. This established the tremendous potential for selling _____ in the Black community.

4. Mamie Smith's recording opportunity came about because _____ _____, a nationally famous White pop singer became ill.

5. Fletcher Henderson and Louis _____ were among those instrumentalists who accompanied Bessie Smith.

6. Some outstanding great male 'Blues' singers include Blind 'Lemon' _____ who traveled and sang for 15 year.

7. McKinley Morganfield is a 'Blues' singer known as _____ Waters.

8. His Blues songs provided a vivid picture of the _____ of the Black people during this period.

9. Some other male 'Blues' singers include _____ Ledbetter, _____ _____ Broonzy and _____ Johnson.

# The Gospel Song

The Black Gospel Song had its birth in the early nineteenth century. It is an outgrowth of the Blues, born out of the sorrow and anguish of the depression of 1929. Gospel songs served to release the tensions and frustrations of the congregation and prepared them to face a new week.

Loneliness, heartache, loss of jobs, lack of proper food and migratory working conditions were prevalent. Soup lines became known to even middle and upper class citizens who had lost all of their savings in the stock market crash of 1929. These conditions led to a strong need for something to hold on to. For many, that something was religion and God. Music similar to the Blues would be needed to stimulate and revive the church services.

The liturgical order of service needed a stronger musical expression which would permit the singer to emotionally testify and sanction or petition for the blessings of God. The Gospel Song was born.

The Gospel Song, a composed religious song, tells the congregation or audience of the singers' particular problems, needs, or desires or of his experiences and knowledge of God. It invokes all those within hearing distance of the singer, who share or have faced the same problems, to join the singers and to sanction or testify along with them. All are directly singing to each other yet indirectly speaking to God, petitioning God or marvelling at the powers of God.

The music of the Gospel Song is exceptionally interesting. It is a composed song with a definite written score yet the printed score merely serves as a general guide line to which the singer or singers must bring his personal religious experiences to in order to express the fervor, intensity and spirit. It is usually joyful and relies on God. Its powerful rhythms and touching melodies often invoke some body movement.

The music of the Gospel song often employs the same devices as the popular style music of the day. Thus there are several styles of Gospel songs:

1. Gospel Pop
2. Gospel Soul
3. Gospel Folk
4. Gospel Blues
5. Gospel Jazz style
6. Gospel Hymn style
7. Gospel Church style (Traditional Gospel style)
8. Gospel Rock style

Wilson Pickett

Some outstanding singers of Gospel music include: James Cleveland, Edwin Hawkin Singers, Andre Crouch, Shirley Ceasar, Sally Marin, Mahalia Jackson, Willia Mae, Ford Smith, Sister Rosetta Tharpe, Clara Ward and Roberta Martin. Some popular singers of Gospel music include Sam Cooke, Wilson Pickett, Staple Singers, Ray Charles, Aretha Franklin.

The Gospel Song also tells of recorded biblical truths or current social truths affecting the performer or performers.

## RECALL

1. The Black Gospel Song is an outgrowth of the _____.

2. The Gospel Song is a composed _____ song.

3. It has a definite written score yet the _____ score merely serves as a general guide line.

4. The music of the Gospel song often employs the same _____ as the popular style music of the day.

5. Some _____ singers also sing Gospel music.

# THOMAS A DORSEY
## 1899

Thomas Andrew Dorsey (1899- ) was born in Villa Ricca, Georgia. His father was a poor preacher and his mother, a strong God-fearing woman. They couldn't afford a musical instrument and Dorsey had to travel five miles three or four times a week to take piano lessons. The family eventually moved to Atlanta where he attended school. He then moved to Chicago, Illinois.

In 1919, he worked at the Gary (Indiana) steel mills and when he wasn't working, he played with a five-piece band that he had organized. The band was always booked and played in the Chicago area for parties and dances. Dorsey often wrote the arrangements for his band. He attended the Chicago Conservatory of Music where he began composing as well as arranging music.

*Thomas A. Dorsey*

Now an excellent Blues and Jazz pianist, in 1921, he joined the Pilgrim Baptist Church in Chicago, and became interested in the music of the church. At a national Baptist Convention which was held at the 8th Regiment Armory in 1921, Dorsey heard a song written by the gospel hymn writer, C.A. Tindley. This song brought the convention to its feet. The sensation and excitement of the music had impressed Dorsey. He now wanted to write this kind of music. His early songs reflect his respect for Tindley.

Charles Albert Tindley (1859-1933) was a methodist minister who was born a slave. He organized a large church in Philadelphia, Pennsylvania that is now called Tindley Temple United Methodist Church.

C.A. Tindley wrote over 50 Gospel hymns which have proved to be among the most popular now sung. They include *Leave It There, Nothing Between, Someday, I Believe It, Bye and Bye When the Morning Comes* and *I'll Overcome Some Day* — which was the inspiration for the Black freedom hymn known as *We Shall Overcome.*

Dorsey was offered and accepted a job with a band called the Whispering Syncopators. The director was Will Walker and one of the members was Lionel Hampton. Dorsey later organized a blues band to play for the Mother of the Blues, Ma Rainey. This band also played for Bessie Smith. He was constantly on tour and became known as Georgia Tom, the Blues pianist and composer.

Dorsey's wife, Nettie, influenced him to return to church music. His did so for a short time but returned to the blues and jazz. This time he teamed up with the famous "Tampa Red" blues singer whose real name was Hudson Whittaker. They wrote *Its Tight Like That* which was a hit.

The crash of the Stock Market in 1929 was financially fatal for Dorsey. He returned to the church and devoted himself solely to writing sacred songs. Not able to find a publisher, Dorsey decided to publish his own songs. At first they were difficult to sell. Dorsey visited church after church to promote his songs. Finally, his perserverance paid off and his songs became very popular. His earlier songs were much like popular style songs with pop-type melodies. His lyrics were direct and to the point. His melodies were haunting and beautiful. His later songs were more rhythmical in a lyrical, folk pop-blues form.

Dorsey created the National Convention of Gospel Singers and developed and trained many Gospel artists, among them Mahalia Jackson, the Queen of Gospel singers; Sallie Martin, singer and Gospel song writer; and James Cleveland, Gospel song writer. Gospel music is now widely accepted and many of Dorsey's songs are known throughout the world. His *Precious Lord, Take My Hand* and *Peace In the Valley* have been translated into almost every language. Dorsey has written many more than 600 songs.

The recording industry of America began to discover the Gospel Song in the 1940's. Sister Rosetta Tharpe, Willie Mae, Ford Smith, Clara Ward, Mahalia Jackson, Roberta Martin, Magnolia Butts and Theodore Fry were influenced by Dorsey who had paved the way for the Gospel Song. He has been the director of the Gospel choirs at Pilgrim Baptist Church in Chicago for forty-five years and has become known as the "Father of Gospel Music." Among the many famous artists that have recorded his music are Tennessee Ernie Ford, Elvis Presley, Roy Rogers and Dale Evans and Aretha Franklin.

Thomas A. Dorsey, the oldest of seven musical children, is the brother of my mother, Bernice Dorsey Johnson who was a composer and pianist herself.

## RECALL

1. Thomas Dorsey had to travel five miles three or four times a week to take _____ lessons.

2. He attended the Chicago _____ _____ _____ and began composing as well as arranging music.

3. Dorsey organized a blues band and played for Ma _____.

4. He became known as _____ _____.

5. The song "_____ _____ _____ _____" has been translated into almost every language.

# MAHALIA JACKSON
## 1911-1972

Mahalia Jackson was born in New Orleans. She later moved to Chicago. From her job as a beautician, she became the 'Queen of Gospel Singers'.

Jackson had a powerful, rich and resonant mezzo voice. She could sing with such vibrance and feeling that she held her audiences spellbound.

Mahalia Jackson received most of her early training from Thomas A. Dorsey (the Father of Gospel Music). When she started recording in the middle '40's, she became internationally known. She gave concerts from Carnegie Hall to the Newport Jazz Festivals. Jackson would only sing Gospel music. She was continuously offered the opportunity to sing Blues or Jazz or popular music, but because of her strong religious beliefs, she said, "I'll only sing for the Lord." She appeared in several movies and has performed at the White House and before royalty and heads of state all over the world.

## RECALL

1. Mahalia Jackson is known as the Queen of
_____ _____.

2. She received most of her early training from
_____ _____.

3. Jackson sang only _____ music.

# MODERN AMERICA
## Rock
## From 1900

# MODERN AMERICA—ROCK
## From 1900
### Rhythm and Blues
### 1941-1950

After World War II (1941-1945), the title 'Blues' gained an added descriptive element, 'Rhythm', and became known as *Rhythm and Blues*. Its appeal was still primarily known to the Black community.

Rhythm and Blues kept the basic Blues structure, but instrumentally added electric guitars (lead and bass), string bass, drums, piano, harmonicas, tenor saxophones, trumpets or trombones. Singers preferred accompaniment by combos, trios and larger groups. This 'City Blues' was very refined with a more intellectual understanding of the society it spoke about. Often the loudness of the accompaniment caused the singers to shout in order to be heard. This new Rhythm and Blues era also produced a definite pulsating beat which was easy to dance to. It fostered such outstanding Rhythm and Blues singers as B. B. King, "Muddy Waters," T. Bone Walker, "Bo" Diddley, Jimmy Witherspoon and Louis Jordan.

Louis Jordan was one of the most influential Rhythm and Blues contributors. He established a place for the electric organ and the saxophone in the Blues. His group, the Tympani Five, played with a jumpy, pulsating rhythm and high-lighted their music with catchy Blues lyrics with sheer wit and outstanding solo passages. Jordan's Rhythm and Blues music created an effect just like the refined refined interplay between voice and instrument in the classically composed art song.

The Blues lyrics, accompaniment, and singing of Louis Jordan combined to create a single mood or effect. Everyone who heard his style was moved by not only the rhythm, but also the unusually clever and witty (often sarcastic) lyrics and beautiful moving instrumental solo passages.

T. Bone Walker contributed to this Blues era with his fantastic mastery of guitar techniques. He also made use of larger bands. His style influenced B. B. King and many others. The vocal and instrumental sounds of Rhythm and Blues paved the way for the 'Rock and Rollers' of the 1950's.

1. After World War II, the 'Blues' gained an added descriptive element, _____.

2. Singers preferred accompaniments by _____.

3. This new Rhythm and Blues Era produced a definite _____ beat.

4. _____ _____ was one of the most influential Rhythm and Blues contributors.

# Early Rock and Roll

About 1950 the large network radio show began to vanish. They had been quite costly and the growth of television and its popularity made them obsolete. In addition, disc jockeys became extremely popular.

The use of magnetic tapes greatly reduced the cost of making records and many new independent record companies were created. New writers appeared and were permitted to join Broadcast Music Incorporated (BMI) which protected their broadcasting and television royalties and rights. BMI was founded to compete with ASCAP (American Society of Composers, Authors and Publishers) which limited membership at the time. Country-Western and Rhythm and Blues artists could now participate through their BMI membership.

The younger record buyers of this period were financially able to purchase records and were very vocal about social issues.

The year 1954 began the era that was to end racially segregated music, that is, 'Black popular music', as it was called, which was generally played and recorded for the Black community. 'White popular music' was played and

Allan Freed

recorded for the White community. Alan Freed, a radio disc jockey, started producing concerts in 1951. He held them in large auditoriums (even ball parks) where he featured several known Black groups and artists. In his effort to create enthusiasm and stimulate ticket sales, he began to promote his concerts with a catchy phrase that had been used by the Rhythm and Blues artists of that time, 'Rock and Roll.' Much to Freed's surprise and pleasure,

the shows were well-attended by both Black and White teenagers.

When Rhythm and Blues was played on White stations or the Hit Parade, they frequently used a White 'cover' group or cover artist. Cover groups were recording groups, other than the original artist, who re-recorded the original version in an attempt to cover or outsell the original. Some examples of such cover versions around 1954 were:

| SONG | ORIGINAL ARTIST | COVER ARTIST |
|------|-----------------|--------------|
| *Ain't That A Shame* | Fats Domino | Pat Boone |
| *Tweedly Dee* | La Verne Baker | Georgia Gibbs |
| *Sh-Boom* | Chords | Crew Cuts |

The public was beginning to take an interest in the competition between the cover versions and the original. For example, La Verne Baker's original version of *Tweedly Dee* outsold Georgia Gibbs' cover version.

A single mood (words, music and powerful beat) had been combined in Rhythm and Blues music. This created a unique impact on the listener. It was not long before this style of music really replaced the Pop music styles which had been dominant. For almost twenty years, this now acceptable Rhythm and Blues music which had been labled Rock and Roll by Alan Freed, related to the young people of the time far better than Pop. It had a heavy, danceable

Little Richard

beat; lyrics which spoke of things young people would know about, were experiencing or could identify with; and the deep intense personal feelings of the performer (usually referred to as 'soul') who maintained a vitally close relationship with his accompaniment.

It is impossible to identify all of the outstanding artists of the period, but one that should be remembered is Little Richard. His emotional song stylings as reflected in his big hits *Tutti Frutti, Good Golly Miss Molly,* and *Rip It Up,* brought the Rock and Roll Era into being. His forceful dynamic style influenced later artists such as the Beatles, Wilson Pickett, Otis Redding and James Brown.

Another influential artist of the period was Chuck Berry (1926-  ). His music and lyrics related well to young people by talking about things that affected them. Berry's big hits were *School Days, Sweet Little Sixteen* and *Roll Over Beethoven.* His music influenced both the Beatles and the Rolling Stones, who began their first musical performances with Chuck Berry's songs.

Bill Haley

Then there was Bill Haley (1925-   ) and His Comets who appeared in the film *Rock Around the Clock* in 1953. Haley tried not to use a cover sound and was the first successful White Rock and Roll artist with his own style. He added drums, Spanish electrical guitar and tenor saxophone to the accompaniment. His biggest hits were *Rock Around the Clock* and *Shake, Rattle and Roll.*

Other outstanding Rock and Roll artists were Fats Domino, Jerry Lee Lewis, Pat Boone, Ricky Nelson, Buddy Holly and Bobby Darin.

The first successful superstar of Rock and Roll to remain consistently popular was Elvis Presley. He was popular on both the Rhythm and Blues and the Country-Western charts in 1956 with his *Heartbreak Hotel* and *You Ain't Nothin' But a Hound Dog.* Recordings that were popular with fans of both styles were called 'crossover' hits.

Elvis Presley

Presley's singing and dancing combined Black body movements and shouts with the Country-Western nasal twang and set almost all females to screaming and jumping in the aisles. They seemed almost possessed. He was what you might call 'wildly successful'. His manner of dress, long hair, side burns, dancing body movements and guitar postures caused an uproar in a more conservative America.

By 1957, many White artists were trying to record Rock music with a true Black sound. The cover versions which imitated Black artists were fading out. Country-Western artists were influenced by this new opportunity. Many of them began to record in this new vein. Among them were Jerry Lee Lewis, Carl Perkins, Buddy Knox and the Everly Brothers. This music took on the title of 'rock-a-billy'.

The national music charts now also included not only Pop but Rhythm and Blues and Country-Western music. The Rock and Roll movement lasted for about eight years and ended in 1958.

### RECALL

1. The year 1954 began the era that was to end _____ _____ music.

2. _____ _____, a radio disc jockey, started producing concerts in 1951.

3. He began to promote his concerts with a catchy phrase, _____ _____ _____.

4. _____ _____ were recording groups other than the original artists.

5. _____ _____ influenced the Rolling Stones.

6. Bill Haley and his _____ was the first successful white rock and roll artist with his own style.

7. _____ _____ singing and dancing combined Black body movements and shouts with the Country-Western nasal twang.

8. By 1957 the _____ versions which imitated Black artists were fading out.

# Lip Sync Artists

The advent of television created a new type of performer. Singers or instrumentalists were chosen mostly because of their attractive physical appearance. The promoters for record companies felt it was imperative for the singer or instrumentalist to look young and attractive on television. When these artists recorded in the studios, technicians were depended upon to improve or develop any sounds necessary to improve the performance.

The artist was then, of course, expected to make television appearances to promote his records. But what had been done by the technicians on their recordings in the studios could not be duplicated on most live television shows.

A new technique was used called 'Lip-Sync,' (lip synchronizaton). The singer simply moved his lips without making a sound while the record played.

Most of the records of this era were associated with particular dances created by the record companies, such as the Fish and the Slop. Live dancing on television became popular.

# Disc Jockeys

With the popularity of the disc jockey, a system known as 'payola' developed. Many disc jockeys were used by record companies as agents to promote their records, as consultants and in various other promotional and money-making positions.

Many of the station programmers, along with many disc jockeys, received cash donations to influence their programming and supporting of certain records. Soon the name Rock and Roll became associated with payola. This practice became so prevalent that a senate investigation into such unfair trade practice resulted. Payola scandals caused a large drop in the sales of Rock and Roll records.

**RECALL**

1. The advent of televison created a new type of _____.

2. When these artists recorded in the studios, _____ were depended on.

3. The new technique was called _____ _____.

4. With the popularity of the disc jockey, a system known as _____ developed.

5. Soon the music style called _____ _____ _____ became associated with payola.

# The 60's
# The Twist and Surf Music

The early '60's saw the beginning of Rock. Performers used a soft Rock beat. Chubby Checker ushered in the Twist in 1961. His recording, *Let's Do the Twist,* accompanied by the dance, the Twist, exhibited a steady beat which was no longer as hard a beat as the earlier Rock and Roll beat.

The Twist was followed, in 1962, by the sounds of the Beach Boys from California. The Beach Boys used four and five part harmony with a Rock beat. They also made use of reverberating guitar effects. The lyrics of their music spoke of surfing and hot-rod racing. This sound became known as the Surf-sound. Other California groups, such as Jan and Dean with *Surf City*, also developed this style.

The California sounds soon led to Folk and Psychedelic (acid) Rock and the use of electronic music. Drugs soon infiltrated the lives of many young people. Music and lyrics seemed to aid the individual's experience while under the influence of drugs who seemed to ignore the disasters of addiction. With *Eight Miles High* by the Byrds, interest in this type of music increased. The Doors also believed in releasing emotions by whatever stimulus necessary. Their big hit was *Light My Fire*. By 1965, the use of strobe lights, projectors, films and other audio-visual aids became a apart of the San Francisco musical scene. Music now included a visual effect to increase psychedelic experiences. Large bands were popular. Some of these groups were the Grateful Dead, Country Joe and the Fish, the Jefferson Airplane, Moby Grape and Big Brother and the Holding Company. They mostly played for dances and presented their shows containing all of the audio-visual effects.

After 1965, these shows faded out as the groups began performing primarily for concerts and exhibited their individualized styles. Appearing were not only bands but also performers such as Janis Joplin.

Then Frank Zappa and the group called The Mothers of Invention recorded *Freak Out*. This record encouraged the relaxing of the dress code and social traditions. It was a combination of Rock, electronic music and some classical motifs with satirical lyrics. Zappa did Rock arrangements of some works by Stravinsky, Mozart and others.

# The Folk Movement

The earlier easy lyrics about surfing and hot-rod car rides began to disappear. College students were becoming more concerned about the social conditions of the time. They had heard and seen enough of teenage songs and catchy dances. The social confusion of the times led them back to a simple mode of expression from the folk heritage. Harry Belafonte brought attention to the Folk Movement.

Harry Belafonte, Jr., is a composer, author, producer and singer who was born in New York City on March 1, 1927. He grew up in Jamaica but attended the New York City Dramatic Workshop. Belafonte became one of the most popular folk singers of our time, appearing on television, in nightclubs, theatres, films and on records.

Other artists of the Folk Movement included the Kingston Trio, The Limelighters, The Chad Mitchell Trio, Peter, Paul and Mary, Judy Collins, Leon Bibb, Pete Seeger, Charlie Rich, Joan Baez, Simon and Garfunkel and Josh White.

## BOB DYLAN

Bob Dylan introduced Folk Rock. Dylan is considered a great Rock poet. One of his earliest songs, *Blowin' in the Wind*, became the battle cry song for many protest groups. His poems and music usually criticized racism and injustices to people.

Folk Rock is just what the name implies—folk songs using simple melodies or tunes with a Rock beat. These are protest songs and songs of personal testimony. Some artists are the Byrds, Sonny and Cher, Simon and Garfunkel, John Denver, Neil Young, James Taylor, Crosby, Stills and Nash and the Mamas and the Papas.

The beginning of the '60's also saw a revival of popular Jazz music using close harmony, smooth sound and only slight improvisation. There was a revival of several old tunes. This music had elements of early Black quartet style singing.

Some artist are the Platters, the Four Freshmen, The Hi-Lows and the Diamonds.

## RECALL

1. The early '60's saw the beginning of _____.

2. Chubby Checker ushered in the _____.

3. By 1965, music included a _____ effect.

4. _____ _____ and the group called the Mothers of Invention recorded *Freak Out*.

5. _____ _____ brought attention to the Folk Movement.

6. _____ introduced Folk Rock.

7. One of his earliest songs, "_____ _____ _____ _____", became the battle cry song for many protest groups.

8. The beginning of the '60's also saw a revival of popular _____ music.

## THE BEATLES

In 1964, the Beatles, a new group from England, came to America. The Beatles offered a new Rock sound. It was a change from the earlier Rock music which spoke of protest, drugs, sex and revolution. These four young men were exciting to young people. Girls fainted, screamed and became so emotional that they often had to be carried out. One of their earliest soft subdued Rock tunes was *I Wanna Hold Your Hand*. It sold millions.

The Beatles were constantly at the top of the Pop charts in America and were, without doubt, the leading Rock group. They were also the most versatile group in the Rock movement with the ability to change and create new styles.

When they first came to America during 1964, they showed an American influence in their music. There could be no doubt that the Beatles had been listening to, and influenced by, Little Richard, Chuck Berry, Elvis Presley, The Isley Brothers and others.

Two members of the Beatles, Paul McCartney and John Lennon, wrote most of their numbers. Ringo Starr and George Harrison completed the foursome.

The earlier songs were simple in melody and text. There was little part singing; it was mostly unison and they offered a subdued emotional type of screaming. The guitar and drum accompaniments seldom stood out above the melody.

The Beatles used a Rhythm and Blues style on their record *She's A Woman* and Chuck Berry's *Roll Over Beethoven*. The American Rock-a-billy style was used in *Words of Love* and the popular American Folk Movement style in *I'll Follow the Sun*.

During the middle sixties, the Beatles used a ballad style as reflected in their recording of *Yesterday*. The accompaniment made use of string octet and cello.

During 1967-1968 they made use of Baroque Rock (the addition of the Rock beat to Baroque music). The accompaniments now included full orchestra, various ensemble arrangments and chamber quartets. An example is *In My Life*.

'Skiffle' music was also used by the Beatles. Skiffle music was created in England. Lonnie Donegan is generally recognized as the originator of this type of Rock. Skiffle music is simply a song in narrative form with a skipping beat rather than a Rock beat. The acoustical guitar maintains the rhythm.

Another type of Rock made use of by the Beatles was 'Raga Rock'. Raga Rock uses music of the Far East (India, etc.). The Raga are individual melodic units which express a distinct mood or emotion. The rhythms are free but complicated. The Beatles combined this Far East music with a Rock beat. They made use of Far East instruments, the most prominent being the sitar. An example of Raga Rock would be *Love To You.*

Still another type of Rock was used by the Beatles was Psychedelic Rock. Psychedelic Rock had its beginning in San Francisco. The music is loosely organized and has no definite time limit. Some compositions last twenty minutes or longer. The text of this music spoke of mystical thinking, philosophies, ideas and the hippie life style. The Beatles' recording of *Yellow Submarine* is an example of Psychedelic Rock.

They Beatles were now beginning to move in the direction of music which could not be performed live. The

*Sgt. Pepper's Lonely Hearts Club Band* (1967) included noise makers, electronic equipment, computers, organ distortions and gimmicks that now firmly established their versatile musicianship. They had become a group with an unrecognizable style, but only because they had achieved success with so many.

Their album, *The Beatles*, traces the history of Rock styles. The group disbanded in 1970 when Paul McCartney left. They had been the leaders in many of the Rock movements. The Beatles grew from a simple group influenced by Americans to a group of representative experimentalists in Rock whose commercial success was unprecedented.

## RECALL

1. In 1964, the _____, a new group from England, came to America.

2. They were the most _____ group in the rock movement.

3. Paul McCartney and _____

_____ wrote most of their numbers.

4. Name three different types of Rock the Beatles used:
   1) _____
   2) _____
   3) _____

## ROLLING STONES

The mid sixties (1964-1967) saw a long list of Rock artists arriving in America from Britain. The most popular group was the Rolling Stones.

The Rolling Stones were strongly influenced by the American Black Rhythm and Blues artist and their styles. They patterned their songs after the artist they most admired—"Bo" Diddley, Chuck Berry and Blues singers like Howlin' Wolf and "Muddy Waters." They were also impressed by contemporary Rhythm and Blues artists like Marvin Gaye, Otis Redding, Wilson Pickett and Billy Preston.

The Stones talked about freedom and inhibiting social customs. To those young people who were politically dissatisfied, the music of the Rolling Stones represented their position. The Stones did change their musical style about 1968 to music with an oriental flavor. This was short-lived and they reverted back to the music that spoke of social conditions.

The Stones' music had a stonger and rougher sound than the Beatles. Mick Jagger was the lead singer and some of their big hits were: *Satisfaction, 2,000 Light Years From Home, You Can't Always Get What You Want* and *Get Off My Cloud.*

Some other British artists performing in America during this period were groups called Herman and His Hermits, Chad and Jeremy, the Dave Clark Five, The Yardbirds, Moody Blues and Gerry and the Pacemakers; and soloists named Tom Jones, Petula Clark, Dusty Springfield and Donovan.

Most of these groups used elements of American Black music and styles. The Yardbirds used elements of Jazz They also made use of the distortion booster (a box placed between the amplifier and the guitar). This gave the guitar a new sound with a sort of wailing effect. The vogue seems to have been—listen to American artists (especially Black Rhythm and Blues artists) and imitate some of the style.

## RECALL

1. The Rolling Stones were strongly influenced by the American Black _____ and _____ artists and style.

2. The Stones' music had a stronger and

_____ sound than the Beatles.

3. Name two other groups of British artists who performed in America during that time:
   1) _____
   2) _____

# Hard Rock

'Hard Rock' is a sound with a hard beat developed in Los Angeles in 1966 and 1967. Music was played at the fullest volume possible. It had a hard and forceful, driving beat. The speed ranged from medium fast to fast. Groups using this Hard Rock music were The Doors, The Who, Steppenwolf and the Jimmi Hendrix Experience.

The instruments used were determined by the group but were basically the electric piano, the electric organ, drums and guitar.

The momentous social revolution for freedom had now broken loose. It included the casting aside of inhibitions and encumberances — to free inner feelings and sensations. This philosophy represented the thinking of The Doors.

Their most popular hit was *Light My Fire.* The Doors did a little more than perform music. Their vocalist, Jim Morrison, used some theatrics.

The Who, another English group, wrote the Rock Opera *Tommy* in 1969. They equalized the volume by balancing instruments and voice. At the end of their performance they would smash their instruments as part of the act.

Another group was The Cream. This Rock band played the Blues and was greatly influenced by B. B. King and "Muddy Waters." The Cream used no single soloist: all three were soloists. They improvised simultaneously and had little regard for any lyrics or message. Their emphasis was on their playing.

# Shock Rock

Jimmi Hendrix was not content with just Hard Rock. He wanted to go beyond this type of Rock. Hendrix called his entire performance *The Jimmi Hendrix Experience.*

An experience it was! He played a wild, super loud Rock type music using distortion and electrical amplification. All the performers seemed to let their feelings, from love to hostility, be expressed through long solo improvisation. Hendrix ended his performance by setting fire to his guitar. This type of Rock became known as 'Shock Rock.'

Hendrix was a fantastic showman and his guitar technique displayed virtuosity unparalleled.

**RECALL**

1. A sound with a _____ beat developed in Los Angeles in 1966 and 1967.
2. Music was played at the _____ volume possible.
3. The Who wrote a rock opera "_____".
4. The _____ were influenced by B. B. King and Muddy Waters.
5. _____ _____ was not content with just Hard Rock.
6. This type of rock became known as _____ Rock.

# Soul Rock

Stars like B. B. King, "Muddy Waters" and "Bo" Diddley were not fully accepted in America's musical circles. B.B. King, among others, had been playing in small Black clubs and lounges for years, receiving nominal salaries. It was their influence on the Beatles, Rolling Stones and other White groups that finally brought them their own past due recognition. The social revolution which was fighting for equality and integration soon led Blacks to use the word 'Soul'. It was used to describe art, people, action or ideas

sympathetic to the ideals of freedom of human emotion and spirit. It meant not only music from the heart, but also derived from personal experience.

Ray Charles (1932-  ) was a major figure in creating and developing an awareness of soul. Ray Charles learned his music in braille. Although blind, he performs on the piano with the dexterity exceeding many sighted pianists. Charles combined Gospel music and Blues with a country flavor. Early in his career, he played in a Rhythm and Blues hillbilly band. This was the first combination of sacred and popular idioms on a record.

James Brown combined some of these idioms of Black preachers' 'shout' style with an intense emotional, guttural sound accompanied by multi-complex rhythms. This style combined with his unusual ability to dance with electrifying speed using smooth, quick steps and rhythmic precision was very influential on the Rock Movement.

Brown, who started out singing ballads like *Georgia,* soon developed his own style which again, like Charles, brought to Rock some elements of Black liturgical music and preaching styles.

Brown's hit *Say It Loud, I'm Black and I'm Proud* became a national anthem for Black citizens during the height of the Civil Rights Movement. This single record not only boosted the Black's dignity and self-respect but also revealed to many Whites in the business world the

*B.B. King*

necessity for creating products and materials for Blacks. Black needs in cosmetics, dolls, advertising and other major areas now began to be important.

Brown's singing has been called 'Raw Soul' and he has been labeled 'Soul Brother No. 1'.

1. _____ _____ was a major figure in creating and developing _____.

2. Charles combined _____ music and Blues in a country flavor.

3. Like Charles, James Brown brought to Rock some elements of Black _____ music.

4. James Brown's singing has been called _____ Soul.

*James Brown*

# Motown (Soul)

During the early '60's, the Black population in America was still on the edge of social equality. The influence of the many Rock styles brought out the Black performer to participate in his own musical heritage.

Barry Gordy, who had been a production line worker, was the founder and developer of the first successful Black record company. The Motown Record Company in Detroit, Michigan, engaged artists such as Smokey

*Smokey Robinson*

Robinson and the Miracles (Smokey also composed most of the songs and was later to become vice-president of Motown), The Temptations, The Four Tops, Martha and the Vandellas, The Marvelettes, The Supremes, then Diana Ross and the Supremes, Dionne Warwick, Stevie Wonder and later the famed Jackson Five.

The sounds produced by Motown were of Rhythm and Blues, Pop and Gospel and a new type Ballad. Each artist-group had its own musical identity and flavor. And one major characteristic of Motown artists was their dress. They had gowns and suits, mostly formal and specially designed. Their mode of dress was equally as important as their singing. The words, music and presentation by the Motown groups and artists was thrilling to hear and see. They created a mood of excitement. The response by the public was overwhelming and their records soon took over the top spots on the American Soul Charts.

Motown instrumentation differed from most White groups because the full orchestra was used. This helped revive an interest in the use of string instruments.

Although the political fight for equal rights and first class citizenship for Blacks was going on, this was not reflected in Motown lyrics. The revolutionary language speaking about drugs, sex and revolution used by many White Rock groups was seldom evident in Motown songs. Motown music chose to speak of the excitement and problems of love affairs or everyday living. For example, Smokey Robinson's, *Baby, Baby Don't Cry;* Diana Ross and the Supremes', *Ain't No Mountain High Enough* and The Jackson Five, *I'll Be There.*

When a Motown artist was heard on a record, it was a smooth and exciting combination of Rhythm and Blues, Pop and Gospel and Ballad style. The audience could deal with and accept the language because no protest or political issues were involved.

When one saw a Motown artist, he saw costuming, dancing and singing usually accompanied by a full orchestra. The excitement and sensationalism were overwhelming.

Motown has now expanded from Detroit to Los Angeles where its activities have also included the production of motion pictures. Motown sound was the greatest company sound of the 1960 Rock-Soul Movement.

1. Barry Gordy was the founder and developer of the _____ Record Company.
2. Each Motown artist-group had its own _____ identity.
3. Motown instrumentation differed from most White groups because the full _____ was used.

4. Although the political fight for Blacks was going on, this _____ reflected in Motown music.
5. When a Motown artist was heard on a record, it was a smooth and exciting combination of _____, pop and gospel and ballad style.

# The Memphis Sound

During the late sixties, Memphis became the Soul Capitol. The sounds of Memphis seemed fuller and heavier than the Motown sound. Artists like Wilson Pickett, Joe Tex, the late Otis Redding, Ike and Tina Turner and Aretha Franklin combined Blues with Gospel music. They used unstrained improvisation and soulful cries. Their music was so compelling that people cried, smiled, shouted and became totally involved.

Aretha Franklin, the 'Queen of Soul,' has an unusual vocal range. Her fervor, intensity, vigor and feeling are apparent from her first sound. Aretha is the daughter of a Baptist minister and sings not just a song but a total experience. The audience lives each moment of the song with her.

She is a composer, pianist and performer and has remained at the top of the charts for many years. She sings Jazz and Scats equally well. She can also sing Gospel music and has the understanding and style that preserves the true Gospel sound whenever she sings it.

Otis Redding

Aretha Franklin

1. During the late sixties, _____ became the Soul Capitol.
2. The artists used _____ improvisation and soulful cries.

3. _____ _____ is the Queen of Soul.

# The Mixing of Styles and Forms

In 1969 and 1970 evidence of another change in the Rock Movement was sensed. Rock was trying to return to its earlier styles. Artists began to use new sounds in old styles. Many major groups recorded using the simple pure Rock forms of Rock and Roll and Rhythm and Blues.

B. B. King's, *The Thrill is Gone* and Blood, Sweat and Tears', *Variations on a Theme by Eric Satie* and the Rolling Stones', *Beggar's Banquet* are prime examples.

In the 1970's Rock completely reflects the combined styles and forms. There appears to be a return to Jazz and a return to Blues. Extra musical effects like the synthesizer and some exciting choreography for huge ball park size concerts have led some Rock groups into almost theatrical productions such as Alice Cooper or the Shock Rock Movement.

David Bowie and his religious music of the church now reflects a Rock beat. Groups like Andrew Crouch, James Cleveland and major recording artists like Aretha Franklin are recording Gospel music with the same accompaniment that a popular Rock recording group would use. Some White singers are now singing in the Black style and many White Gospel accompanists have learned the Gospel style; some Black singers have mastered the White styles; some Jazz singers are 'making a comeback' and are becoming popular.

The big band sounds are being heard and welcomed by a generation who has never heard them before. Even some of the Swing Era dances have been revived and become "new." The Pointer Sister are symbolic in dress and song of a Jazz interest in earlier style. There is evidence of Latin American rhythm in the sounds of Burt Bacharach. He seems to have drawn from all sources to form his own popular Rock sound.

Where will Rock go? Who knows—but its beat and its styles will continue in some manner.

The genius of giant composers and performers like Stevie Wonder, Elton John, John Denver, Neil Diamond, Judy Collins, Melissa Manchester, Janis Ian, Carly Simon, Joni Mitchell, Paul Simon, James Taylor, Neil Sedaka and Chick Corea and bands like Chicago, Adam Clayton Thomas and Blood, Sweat and Tears will follow the stream of creation which their social surroundings dictate.

Stevie Wonder

# The Pulse

# The Pulse

It is probably impossible for us to learn all of the history of music in one lifetime. We certainly couldn't do it in one year or in one book. But with this introduction, it is my hope that you can spot the music and musicians who will involve your heart in the pulse of music during each historical period. With the pulse will come love of music through understanding. Man and the pulse of his music are inseparable. As the pulse of our music changes, we will change.

The famous Greek philosopher Plato sensed this back in 500 B.C.—"A change to a new type of music is something to beware of as a hazard of all our fortunes. For the modes of music are never disturbed without unsettling of the fundamental political and social conventions."

I wish you all of the joy of a long life accompanied by the pulse of music—

**Lena McLin**